# Know Yourself, Co-workers and Your Organization

# KNOW YOURSELF, CO-WORKERS AND YOUR ORGANIZATION

———————— ◆ ————————

## Get Focused On: Personality, Careers and Managing People

*Jack A. Juchnowski, M.A.*

iUniverse Star
New York   Lincoln   Shanghai

**Know Yourself, Co-workers and Your Organization**
**Get Focused On: Personality, Careers and Managing People**

iUniverse Star
an iUniverse, Inc. imprint

For information address:
iUniverse, Inc.
2021 Pine Lake Road, Suite 100
Lincoln, NE 68512
www.iuniverse.com

ISBN: 0-595-29727-7

Printed in the United States of America

For my dad, Joseph S. Juchnowski, who would be very proud and *surprised*, Ms. Skip Jamison who is *very* excited and encouraged me throughout this entire project, and my immediate family: Linda and Paul Kadis; Joseph and Carol Juchnowski; Jan, Donna, Jessie and Jackie Juchnowski; Debbie, Sean, Beth and Alex McCoy.

For Marko Sfilijog, who offered me unconditional encouragement and support to pursue my education when I worked for him as a crystal grower. Also, for Lenny.

Finally, for Panda, our wonder dog.

# CONTENTS

———————◆———————

# LIST OF TABLES

◆

# PREFACE

This book is the culmination of an effort to significantly expand upon existing descriptive information associated with the Holland theory of personality and work environments. It flows from my inescapable interest in this theory and near compulsion to translate my many years of observing people and management consulting work into a practical volume based upon John Holland's work. I am deeply appreciative of Dr. Holland's remarkable contribution to vocational and industrial psychology as well as the field of psychology as a whole. I hope anyone familiar with the Holland theory finds this book illuminating and is inspired to a deeper understanding and application of it in their work. One last hope is that anyone becoming acquainted with Dr. Holland's work for the first time through this book use it wisely to select jobs, careers, live more satisfying lives, and exhibit greater tolerance for people who are different from themselves.

# ACKNOWLEDGEMENTS

◆

I would like to acknowledge the following people in alphabetic order who reviewed the original manuscript for this book, offered editorial suggestions, provided encouragement, or exhibited much-needed enthusiasm for this undertaking: Rick Bastion, M.A., Ted Dorfman, M.A., Dave Gilmore, Ph.D., Bruce Harris, Ph.D., Melinda Adams Merino, Jim Schuerger, Ph.D., and Travis White, Ph.D.

A special acknowledgement to Dr. John L. Holland. Without his theory, this book would not exist.

I would also like to acknowledge Ms. Skip Jamison who helped me bring *Know Yourself* to this point, and thank the folks at iUniverse, Inc., who were involved with this project, notably Pam Anderson who was my Publishing Services Associate and Denise, my copyeditor.

I wish to acknowledge the city of Cleveland, Ohio where I was born, grew up and shaped. This fine city is quietly growing and positioning itself for a rebirth that I look forward to witnessing.

I would like to acknowledge Cleveland State University for the education it provided me.

Finally, thanks to the Lake County (Ohio) Metroparks, particularly Hogback Ridge Reservation, where I spent many hours writing, editing and revising the manuscript for this book. Completing this work in such wonderful surroundings certainly made the task easier (while giving me a chance to take a hike when I needed a break).

# INTRODUCTION

————————— ◆ —————————

A key goal of this book is to help you learn more about yourself. While assisting you in this process, you will be introduced to a theory of careers and vocational life. Don't be alarmed (if you are prone to be) by the word "theory." This theory is a friendly theory. It's a helpful theory. It's a simple theory. And, most of importantly, it is a powerful theory.

Another goal of this book is to steer you towards finding a job and career that suits your needs—based upon who you are as a person. Coincidentally, the theory I mentioned is also a theory of personality. So, we'll be able to "kill two birds with one stone," so to speak.

A final goal of this book is to help you, as a manager, better understand people on your team and, in turn, help them reach their potential on the job. You will be able to accomplish this by applying what you learn about people and their personalities throughout this book.

At this point, I would suppose you are wondering, "What is this theory, anyhow?" Let's get to it.

A psychologist by the name of John Holland formulated a way of classifying people. This classification system was an outgrowth of work Holland and other psychologists performed in the area of "interest measurement." Holland proposed that people with similar interests work in the same or similar fields. Conversely, people with different interests work in different fields. Beyond this, Holland demonstrated that people of similar interests shared a number of other characteristics. These would include such things as skills, abilities, personality attributes and, dislikes, among others. Holland also proposed that people could be classified according to six different themes or types.

Sounds pretty simple—even "common-sensical." True enough. Nevertheless, this classification system was a **large** step forward in the field of vocational counseling because it lead to a sensible, logical way of classifying both jobs and careers as well as *people* working in those jobs and careers.

The advantage of Holland's approach over others is that it is a concise formulation without being simplistic or needlessly complex. Non-psychologists certainly find it easy to understand and use—as you will soon discover. In fact, John Holland made a specific point of outlining all aspects of his theory in easily understood language.

There is a final point I wish to make before you move ahead with learning about Holland's theory and *yourself.* It is that this is **the theory** in the vocational and career fields. No other past or current theory of vocations has generated the attention and scientific research attributed to Holland's. Consequently, the Holland theory has stood up incredibly well to the rigors of critical review and research aimed at testing its soundness and usefulness. At this point in time, there has been a tremendous amount of investigation and study in support of its concepts.

Yet, surprisingly, Holland's theory has escaped widespread recognition beyond the professionals who rely heavily upon it to conduct research, teach about career counseling, or provide such counseling. Non-professionals who have heard of the Holland types have probably done so by seeking the services of a vocational counselor or, perhaps, completing a course in college covering personality measurement and assessment. A hindrance to creating broad interest in this theory has been the lack of a book that fully elaborates each theme along with the nature of the six Holland work environments.

Thus, in a real sense, *Know Yourself* is the first attempt to bring the power of the Holland theory to the attention of the general public or working women and men. It also represents the only book to fully describe the unique characteristics of the fifteen Holland pairs (or dyads) along with the six Holland work environments. In addition, this book significantly expands upon existing descriptions of the six Holland personality types. In fact, the above are the specific contributions of *Know Yourself* to the fields of vocational and personality psychology.

So, here you have it; an elaboration of John Holland's types and work environments and a guide for using that information to better understand yourself, your coworkers, and making satisfying career decisions. It is my belief everyone can find gratifying, enjoyable work, and the best place for *themselves* to perform it. Holland's theory as presented within this book will help you do exactly that.

◆

# Part One

# LEARNING ABOUT YOURSELF

## The Holland Theory: The basics

If the Holland theory is viewed from a limited perspective, it is seen as a theory of careers, vocations and interests. That is, it provides a basis for understanding the relationship(s) between people's interests and the diversity of careers from which they have to choose. It also offers people a solid means for narrowing down their vocational or occupational choices.

Yet, if Holland's theory is looked at from a broader perspective, it is truly a theory of personality as well. In fact, it is powerful in its ability to describe people while capturing a considerable amount of observed human complexity while doing so.

The Holland theory categorizes careers, occupations, job environments, interests and, ultimately, people, into six types or themes. Each theme or type is unique and notably different from the others in terms of its focus, orientation to the world, values, motivations, abilities, et cetera. The themes include Realistic, Investigative, Artistic, Social, Enterprising, and Conventional.

To remember the six themes, John Holland created a word, RIASEC (pronounced RYE-UH-SECK). Each letter in this word represents a single theme.

More importantly, the ordering of the letters in this word reveals much about the relation of each theme to the others. Those "touching each" other have a number of qualities or attributes in common (in addition to, of course, their differences). These are called consistent themes (RI, IA, AS, SE, EC, CR).

Thus, careers, occupations, environments or people can be described as representing a single theme (e.g. a "Realistic occupation or person). In addition, all of these can also be described as combinations of multiple themes (e.g., a "Realistic / Investigative" occupation or a RIA person). By convention, occupations are normally described by a combination of three or fewer themes.

In addition to consistent or complementary themes, there exist inconsistent themes. The most inconsistent themes are those in the word, RIASEC, that are two spaces apart (RS, IE, AC). For practical and theoretical purposes, these pairings (dyads) are *virtual* opposites. That is to say, inconsistent pairs represent themes that possess very different characteristics, abilities, interpersonal styles, work styles, interests, patterns of thinking, et cetera. These dyads share little in common with each other.

Finally, those themes that are one space apart vary in terms of their consistency or relatedness. Certain of them are complementary (e.g., IC, CS) and share a number of common attributes or, at least, are not vastly different on various dimensions of personality, interest, ability, et cetera. Others are non-complementary (e.g., RA, AE) and demonstrate little consistency. When measured on various dimensions, they come across as notably different from each other.

A better way to understand or comprehend the relationship of the six themes to each other is to represent them in a hexagonal configuration, as John Holland did. Below are the Holland themes in such an orientation.

R                    I


C                                        A


E                    S

Notice that if lines are drawn between themes that are *across* from each other, it is clear they are unrelated or dissimilar. Thus, the "opposite-ness" of the RS, IE, and AC pairs are visually (and, geometrically) clear. So too, is the notion of the similarity of themes in close proximity to each other (i.e., those that are adjoining or two spaces apart).

To begin to gain a sense for what each theme is like, the following brief discussion will suffice as an introduction.

The Realistic theme is concerned with things over people. Such individuals are typically down-to-earth and forthright, and often have mechanical abilities and interests. Realistic persons enjoy outside activities and doing things with their hands.

The Investigative theme is concerned with ideas over things and people. They are reserved individuals who often have analytical abilities and scientific interests. They enjoy thinking, problem solving, and doing things with their minds.

The Artistic theme is concerned with creating and using their imagination. They are expressive individuals (verbally, visually, musically or otherwise), who enjoy coming up with new, novel and innovative ideas, and translating them into art, writing, acting, music, et cetera.

The Social theme is concerned with helping and nurturing others. They are friendly, caring individuals who have the ability to deal effectively with people. Social individuals enjoy assisting, caring for, and being of service to others.

The Enterprising theme is concerned with influencing people to achieve valued goals. They are assertive people who enjoy leading, directing and persuading others. Enterprising individuals enjoy competition and are often business oriented.

The Conventional theme is concerned with order, following procedures and doing things properly. They are typically quiet, introverted individuals as well as patient, detail-oriented and often good with numbers. Conventional individuals enjoy activities that allow them to use their computational skills, oftentimes in a business setting.

There you have it! The Holland Theory in a relatively abbreviated (but, not too) format. Simple yet, powerful. Just as promised. Now we are almost ready to **do something** with this information. Almost. Before that, we are going to examine the six themes or personalities in greater depth. As we do, you will begin to *find yourself in Holland's theory.*

# CHAPTER I

◆

# REALISTIC TYPES: "WE LIKE THINGS."

As indicated in the title of this chapter, Realistic types (*Rs*) of people like "things." This is as opposed to their preferring conceptual ideas, being creative, interacting with a lot of different people, leading others or being concerned with order, efficiency and manipulating data. If given a choice, *Rs* would prefer to deal with other people who have a similar preference. This is not to say *Rs* are unable or unwilling to do other things or interact with other types of people. They can, of course. However, they like to stick with their preferences if possible. Yet, *Rs* interests and preferences can take on a variety of forms. So too, can their abilities. Their personalities are also broader than might be inferred from the above comments. Let's take a look at what makes an *R* an *R*.

## Interpersonal style

Realistic types are straightforward and down-to-earth when dealing with others. They are also serious, informal and most comfortable working alone, in small groups or with people whom they know well. *Rs* do not readily extend themselves to others (especially to those they do not know well or feel are at all pretentious or phony), and would not be described as outgoing, gregarious or sociable. Despite the foregoing, *Rs* are not always serious and, in fact, have an earthy sense of humor. However, at times, the *Rs* sense of humor can be a bit coarse or off-color (i.e., "locker-room" humor). In the extreme, some *Rs* can lean toward being loners. This reflects their independent nature and desire to be self-sufficient. Unfortunately, they can also be slow to ask for, and seek help, and may struggle too long on their own with problems for these same reasons.

Oftentimes, *Rs* are brief, direct and to-the-point when speaking and are not especially polished communicators. They speak plainly and are not inclined to talk at great length. *Rs* would much rather say what they think without *thinking,* more than they have to about what they have to say. Some can come across as fairly inarticulate and may struggle to find words to get their thoughts across. In fact, *Rs* can be brief or imprecise conveying information when speaking or writing. This type is not comfortable speaking to groups or making presentations—even to people they know well, or those with similar interests and backgrounds. The idea of the "strong, silent" male is an accurate representation of Realistic men. Yet, whether male or female, the above qualities hold true for *all Rs*.

The selectivity of *Rs* as far as who they choose as friends, makes them difficult for most people to get to know on a personal level. In this regard, they are guarded—even suspicious—of other people and their motives. Compounding this is the fact that *Rs* can be judgmental of people they meet for the first time. They sometimes form strong, negative opinions based upon little information or contact with them. For *Rs*, it is fair to say that a poor initial impression is a lasting one. Similarly, *Rs* can be unforgiving if others let them down. On the other hand, a *positive* initial impression can be equally long lasting. In any case, a person must earn the trust, respect and confidence of the *Rs* over time. Once taken into the *Rs* confidence, others will find they do become much more open.

*Rs* have a need to be alone periodically. That is, continuous contact with people is wearying for them. Therefore, *Rs* need a break after a prolonged period of interaction with people. (This is true for them at work and *off work*.) Of course, getting such a "break" is not always possible. This then can be a source of frustration or stress for *Rs*.

Another quality people notice in *Rs,* is their extreme loyalty to those who pass their scrutiny. Although *Rs* tend to have relatively few friends, they maintain friendships for a long time. Conversely, when someone makes a poor initial impression, lets the *Rs* down or breaches their trust, it can be extremely difficult to regain their "good graces."

The guarded, serious-minded, interpersonal style of the *Rs* can cause them to downplay feelings, (especially "tender" ones) and emotions. As a result, they often overlook their own such feelings and those of others. As parents, supervisors or managers, they are not particularly nurturing. Instead, *Rs* are firm, tough-minded and emotionally controlled or restrained. They can also be quicker to notice and point out flaws or criticize, than praise and encourage. Yet, this does not reflect ill intent on their part. It is merely indicative of the *Rs* style and orientation to the world and people around them.

## Talents, abilities and decision making

The abilities of this type generally fall in the realm of working with "things" rather than people or ideas. This includes physical, mechanical and spatial abilities. Physical abilities revolve around working with one's hands along with strength, agility and endurance. The *Rs* physical agility can often take on the form of athletic ability and skill performing in various sports activities. Mechanical ability is the practical application and translation of physical abilities. This involves understanding how to use a wide range of tools, machinery and equipment to build, repair or construct things. Spatial ability involves the capacity to mentally visualize two-dimensional drawings in the normal three dimensions we live in. This includes being able to accurately read and understand blueprints and what they represent. At a higher level of understanding, mechanical / spatial abilities enter into the realm of physics and engineering capabilities.

Realistic types are often pragmatic problem solvers who use common sense and *their own* past experience and training effectively on the job. They tend to be most adept handling problems that are concrete and straightforward, versus those that are conceptual, theoretical or ambiguous. *Rs* usually learn best through hands-on situations where they are able to gain knowledge by doing, versus reading books or through verbal or classroom instruction. In fact, *Rs* often find classroom settings constricting, boring and uncomfortable.

*Rs* are conservative and cautious in their outlook. Likewise, they are traditionalists who would ascribe to what could be termed "old-fashioned" values and beliefs. They are true to their beliefs and receive strength from them during difficult times. Yet, *Rs* are risk aversive and find change frustrating and upsetting—unless, of course, the reasons for it are practical, clear and sensible. These qualities can also emerge as inflexibility, rigidity and stubbornness in *Rs*. Once they have formed an opinion or made a decision, *Rs* can be unyielding.

In general, *Rs* are weaker in the area of verbal communication skills. They can be too brief relaying information in writing and when speaking. There are also apt to be deficiencies in their word knowledge, use of grammar, syntax, and punctuation. The preference of the *Rs* are to be plain spoken, and not too "fancy" in their choice of words.

In relations with others, *Rs* can assume too much of them. For example, expecting the people around them to think much like themselves or have similar outlooks and values. This can result in *Rs* making notable misjudgments about people—good and bad. Likewise, *Rs* are not especially strong in terms of their social interaction or human relation skills, (they are often direct and no-nonsense-like), nor do they excel at resolving people problems.

Furthermore, *Rs* are not adept at resolving conceptual, ambiguous, theoretical or abstract problems. They find these frustrating to deal with and difficult to grasp. Likewise, *Rs* are seldom creative or original thinkers. Instead, they tend to be conservative in their outlook. This can result in *Rs* resisting change and a lack of innovation in departments or organizations managed by them.

## Work style and motivational factors

As noted earlier, *Rs* are task oriented and practical minded in their outlook. They prefer to use their time sensibly, while doing something that will yield a tangible result, whether on or off the job. *Rs* proceed through their work in a step-by-step fashion while remaining well focused on the task at hand. Moreover, they are most comfortable and perform best in structured environments where everyone's role, particularly their own, is clear-cut and specific. *Rs* are apt to feel frustration if such is not the case, or expectations and goals are ill-defined or too general.

*Rs* do not enjoy, nor do they often engage, in reflective (i.e., introspective) activities or those that involve contemplation. In light of this, *Rs* are ill-suited to positions requiring abstract or conceptual thinking. Instead, they are concrete in their outlook and ways of thinking. The latter attribute, and *Rs* non-emotional style, does help them stay focused on the work they are performing.

On the job, *Rs* are generally disciplined, hard working and reliable. It is not unusual for an *R* employee to arrive earlier than others at work in an effort to be sure they are on time, (provided, of course, they enjoy their work). Thus, *Rs* can be counted on to do what they commit to, and have a strong sense of responsibility. As well, *Rs* stay on top of work they are responsible for completing, and are effective short-range planners.

*Rs* are usually consistent performers who develop sensible work routines for completing recurring tasks. These routines form the basis for organizing and planning their work. *Rs* pay attention to important details and can be "artisan-like" getting their work completed. Yet, this also implies that *Rs* can be too meticulous in some regards. At times, they may exceed requirements on projects—pet projects—or those they find particularly interesting. Likewise, *Rs* can be difficult to please in some regards and may expect too much from others. This is often the case in areas where they are quite skilled and others are not. In such instances, *Rs* can be impatient with coworkers or feel they are just not trying hard enough to do a good job.

## Leadership

*Rs* can be effective in roles where they use their specialized knowledge and experience to direct the efforts of others. *Rs* will assume a leadership role if asked to or when they feel they have reached a sufficient level of proficiency in their job or chosen field. Another basis upon which *Rs* will accept a leadership role, is when their time-in-service, (tenure) with an organization makes them a clear choice over others with less tenure.

When serving in leadership positions, *Rs* can be adept at structuring what must be done. In this regard, their organizational skills and task-focused style help them coordinate projects and keep them on track. They determine the role of everyone on their team and make it clear they expect work to be completed on time and in accord with the guidelines, they or others (usually superiors) have established. *Rs* lead and motivate their team with their own hard working example. Unfortunately, they usually display limited insight into what it takes to get the best performance out of individual team members. Compounding this is the tendency of *Rs* to more readily see and point out flaws in a worker's performance than to offer praise and positive recognition.

*Rs* are no-nonsense leaders who quickly address problems—work, or people related—as they develop. Furthermore, *Rs* believe in and respect the chain of command along with the authority and decisions of superiors. This keeps things orderly, but can also result in their not being open to questions or objections to their decisions from associates. In this regard, *Rs* are often set in their ways. Likewise, their outlook is conservative. This means *Rs* are not inclined to take too many risks in their work, preferring instead, to stick with proven methods and techniques as opposed to innovative approaches.

As leaders, *Rs* are tacticians. That is, they are adept at short-range planning. *Rs* stay well attuned to immediate demands, issues and problems faced by their team. A notable weakness for *Rs* as leaders, is their lack of vision and inability to be sufficiently strategic in their thinking. This is a direct consequence of being so task and results-oriented on the job. They focus mostly on the "here and now," so to speak.

## Interests: occupational and academic

*Rs* enjoy outdoor activities. Many hunt and enjoy fishing, camping and boating as pastimes. Thus, *Rs* typically have an appreciation for nature, though not in an aesthetic, romantic sense. Gardening and farming are also enjoyable to many *Rs*. Along with this, they are often quite involved with the maintenance of their homes, automobiles and private property. Carpentry and woodworking can serve as excellent hobbies for *Rs*.

## <u>Occupational</u>

*Rs* seek jobs that are results, task and "thing" oriented, versus people oriented. They prefer their work and efforts lead to a measurable, observable and practical end result. And, as noted earlier, *Rs* prefer structure in their jobs regarding roles, guidelines, rules, objectives, et cetera. They have a low tolerance for ambiguity and find it frustrating and upsetting. *Rs* are often security-minded. Consequently, they will make a long-term commitment to employers who treat them fairly. Thus, if they enjoy their work and feel respected and treated squarely by their employer, *Rs* are unlikely to jump from job to job.

## Academic

While in high school, *Rs* find vocational education programs or courses more interesting than academic-oriented studies. They are also apt to prefer work-study programs that allow them to learn a skill at school and apply what they learn in a job situation. If *Rs* attend college, they lean towards skill-based, practical programs that prepare students for particular types of work matching their current abilities or interests. *Rs* are most likely to attend a two-year college if it will more quickly get them into the career field of their choice, and happily forego the extra course work required to earn a bachelor's degree.

# College programs that fall within the Realistic theme:

Aeronautical Technology

Agricultural Education

Aircraft Mechanics

Animal Nutrition

Architectural Drafting

Automotive Mechanics

Automotive Technology

Brick Masonry

Business Machine Repair

Carpentry

Cartography

Computer Servicing Technology

Conservation and Regulation

Construction Equipment Operation

Construction Inspection

Cooling and Refrigeration

Dental Laboratory Technology

Diesel Engine Mechanics

Drafting

Emergency Medical Technology

Engineering

Firefighting

Food Packaging

Forestry

Forestry Science

Geological Engineering

Heating & Air Conditioning

Heavy Equipment Repair

Horseshoeing

Industrial Arts

Industrial Technology

Instrumentation Installation

Jewelry Fabrication / Repair

Landscaping

Major Appliance Repair

Materials Engineering

Mechanical Engineering

Mechanical Technologies

Military Technologies

Mining Engineering

Nuclear Power Plant Technology

Oceanography

Optical Technology

Optics

Orthotics / Prosthetics

Petroleum Technology

Plastics Technology

Plumbing

Quality Control Technology

Refrigeration

Renewable Natural Resources

Robotics Technology

Small Appliance Repair

Small Engine Repair

Technical Education

Tool and Die Making

Transportation

Turf Management Science

Ultrasound Technology

Welding Technology

Woodworking

**Self-test**

The following questionnaire is designed to help you determine how closely you match up with the Realistic Holland theme. You will be asked to check off ("√") answers you think describe yourself or match your interests. ***Do not be surprised if you √ many or only a few phrases or words on this questionnaire.*** For each section, honestly respond to the questions. Do not hurry. Move at a comfortable, relaxed pace.

<u>Part 1</u> Directions: Indicate with a √ which of the following phrases describe you on the job or come close to your views.

__    I try to get things done right the first time.

__    I do not waste time chitchatting.

__    I prefer to work on my own.

__    I rely on common sense to make decisions.

__    I am productive at work and do not waste time daydreaming.

__    I prefer a job that leads to some sort of concrete, actual result.

__    If given a choice, I would prefer proven methods over experimental methods.

__    A manager should simply tell unproductive workers to "shape up or ship out."

<u>Part 2</u>  Directions: From the list of words or phrases below, indicate with a √ those that are *descriptive of you.*

__ frank            __ persistent    __ self-reliant        __ to-the-point

__ traditional      __ unsociable    __ can be stubborn __ tough-minded

__ dislike change __ handy         __ pragmatic          __ judgmental

<u>Part 3</u>  Directions: From the list of Occupations and College Majors below, indicate those you think you would enjoy or find interesting with a √. *Do not worry if you lack the expertise or education to excel in these areas.*

__ Cabinetmaker          __ Forester             __ Automotive Engineering

__ Firefighter            __ Mining Technology   __ Construction Supervisor

__ Industrial Arts        __ Drafting             __ Agricultural Education

__ Production Supervisor  __ Electrician          __ Mechanical Engineering

<u>Directions for scoring</u>: Add all of the √s you made in each of the three parts. The total number of √s is your raw score on the Realistic Holland theme. Enter that total score below in the blank on the first line.

My raw score on the Realistic theme is: _____ (Enter your total score)

This score falls within the _____ percentile range. (Refer to chapter 7)

This score falls within the _____ category. (Refer to chapter 7)

## Developmental advice

If your score on the self-test was in the *high* or *average* ranges, you may find some of the suggestions that follow helpful.

If you choose to work on any of these areas, do not attempt to do too much at once. Select *two* or *three* items. Enlist the support and encouragement of persons you respect in this process and seek their feedback and advice periodically.

1)    Make more of an effort to extend yourself to other people at work—take the initiative or first step in doing so.

2)    Demonstrate greater tolerance and understanding for different types of people.

3)    Avoid being too quick to judge other people in a negative way. Look past first impressions of others that are not favorable.

4)    If people offend you or let you down, give them another chance—try to see their perspective.

5)    Before saying exactly what is on your mind when you are frustrated, consider how others might react. Try to be diplomatic when expressing strong opinions or simply withhold comment.

6)    Be open-minded and flexible when presented ideas that are different from your own.

7)    Occasionally question why you do things a certain way. Ask yourself if there might be a better, more innovative approach.

8)    When making decisions, always consider how different options will work out for the long term; six, twelve or more months into the future.

9)    If you supervise people, take time to offer them praise and encouragement. Don't be too critical and learn more about how to motivate employees.

10)    If you supervise others, be patient when teaching or training. Remember, some people need extra coaching or detailed answers and instructions to catch on.

11) Do not struggle on your own with problems too long—seek help promptly.

12) Be sure to arrange leisure time for yourself, instead of working too much or too many hours. This is especially important when you have worked a long stretch of time closely with other people.

## Final comment

If your score on the self-test was in the *high* range, you may need to broaden your interests and become accepting of people who are different from yourself. People characterized by the Social theme would be most different from you in interests, personality and values. Re-read chapter 4 to learn about such people and their interests.

# Chapter 2

◆

# Investigative Types: "We like ideas."

As indicated in the title of this chapter, Investigative types (*Is*) of people like "ideas." This is as opposed to their preferring things, being creative, interacting with many different people, leading others or being concerned with order, efficiency and manipulating data. If given a choice, *Is* would prefer to deal with other people who have a similar preference. This is not to say *Is* are unable or unwilling to do other things or interact with other types of people. They can, of course. However, they like to stick with their preferences if at all possible. Yet, *Is* interests and preferences can take on a variety of forms. So too, can their abilities. Their personalities are also broader than might be inferred by the above comments. Let's take a look at what makes an *I* an *I*.

## Interpersonal style

*Is* are reserved, often understated, courteous and generally cooperative. The latter is especially true when they are able to use their specialized knowledge, expertise or training to assist others. At the same time, *Is* are slow to extend themselves to others they do not know well, and are cautious in new situations.

*Is* lean toward the introspective, reflective and philosophical. In fact, they can be difficult to get to know on a personal, informal level. Yet, as mentioned earlier, *Is* often have strong verbal skills and a good command of the language. So, they can be adept at relaying information to others, particularly in areas they know well (provided they are comfortable with their "audience"). Unfortunately, in this regard, *Is* can be too technical in their orientation. Consequently, they may have difficulty meeting others at their level of understanding when sharing information.

To some people, *Is* may seem to "talk above their heads," which can lead to confusion and frustration for others. This can also convey the impression *Is* are a bit lofty or place themselves above others, which is not necessarily intentional. When it is intentional, it may represent a way for *Is* to prevent others from getting too close to them at an emotional level.

On the job, *Is* are apt to be viewed as intelligent, perhaps aloof (arrogant in extreme cases) but, good sources of information. Thus, they earn respect for what they know, as well as their insight and problem solving abilities. It is gratifying for *Is* to be viewed in this manner. Along these lines, they can be effective in certain types of consultative roles (e.g., specific, technical versus generalized consulting). Likewise, they are apt to perform particularly well in an individual contributor role when their specialized knowledge, skills and training can be utilized. In such roles, *Is* ability to operate independently works in their favor. Moreover, *Is* can be valuable functioning in small teams working to complete or resolve a complex project or problem. They are apt to open up more in such situations and enjoy the diversity of expertise and experience of the various people involved.

## Talents, abilities and decision making

The abilities of the *I*-type generally fall within the realm of working with ideas (analyzing, researching, assessing, predicting, forecasting) rather than things or people. This includes scientific work, abstract and deductive reasoning, and conceptual thinking. *Is* are comfortable dealing with theoretical concepts and are often imaginative in finding solutions. They are usually insightful and adept at grasping and understanding difficult ideas or issues. Of the six Holland themes, *Is* are the most analytical and rational.

*Is* can, however; take their analytical, methodical style too far though. That is, they can be too deliberate, thorough and cautious. This can result in *Is* taking too long to arrive at decisions especially when they are working on interesting, intriguing problems or operating under loose deadlines. Thus, *Is* often function best as problem solvers, time -wise, when they are given a deadline for finding or finalizing solutions. Along similar lines, *Is* are not risk takers, and they move carefully when venturing into the unknown. For this reason, *Is* are unlikely to make mistakes out of haste or reliance upon their instincts. Yet, they can also miss some opportunities due to this.

As noted earlier, *Is* oftentimes have sound verbal skills and a fairly broad vocabulary. Yet, when sharing information, *Is* can err on the side of being too wordy. This flows from their need and desire to be thorough and complete when explaining themselves, which can be frustrating for people (e.g., *Rs* and *Es*) who only want an overview or concise information.

*Is* are often strong with regard to numerical reasoning, mathematical, and statistical abilities. Along with this, many are strategic thinkers and capable of seeing the long-range implications of their decisions. *Is* normally learn quickly compared to other types and are analytical and logical when evaluating information, issues or possibilities. Further, *Is* usually do well in academically oriented learning situations, and where mastery of a particular area or factual information is important.

*Is* are weaker in terms of their social interaction skills (they focus most of their attention on their work and problem solving), and handling practical issues (tending toward making them too complex or failing to see the simple solutions). People problems, not easily resolved using logic, can pose difficulty for *Is*, as they can be too rational and not emotionally sensitive enough. Similarly, *Is* are suspicious of intuitive approaches to decision making, and will discount them if others suggest decisions arrived at by such means.

Another "danger" area for *I*-types is their potential to overlook practical concerns and issues that could get in the way of implementing their sometimes, "elegant" solutions. Such things as cost, time and resource constraints can be left out of their "equation." Thus, in organizations *Is* can be viewed as lacking in business sense or even common sense.

## Work style and motivational factors

*Is* are logical and systematic in their approach to their work. Thus, they take time to ask questions and do their "homework" before beginning any assignment. Similarly, *Is* are often thorough planners who can be comprehensive in developing strategies to achieve objectives. They typically do a fine job anticipating potential problems in advance, and factor this information into their plans. *Is* also have the potential to see how the smaller elements of a project must fit together to complete the overall picture.

Because *Is* are comfortable dealing with ambiguity, goals and objectives need not be carefully spelled out and specific for them to begin their work. Given this, *Is* can operate effectively, even when goals and guidelines are vague versus clear-cut.

The methodical style and preference of the *Is* to be thorough can lead to their being perfectionists when completing projects. This likelihood is noticeably increased when they are working on particularly intriguing and interesting projects. If *Is* are not given firm timelines and guidelines within which to operate, this propensity can become more pronounced and troublesome, resulting in pushed deadlines.

Generally, *Is* are motivated on the job by learning. They want to develop mastery of specific areas of knowledge and information. They will work long, hard and conscientiously to accomplish this goal. In this regard, they are quietly persevering and observant. Autonomy is also important to *Is*. Thus, they want to arrive at their own conclusions and be free from close scrutiny or supervision at work. In addition, *Is* want intellectual challenges, and become bored quickly with mundane, repetitive tasks. Similarly, they can lose interest when a project enters the maintenance or routine stages; that is, the point where learning begins to decrease.

## Leadership

*Is* do not aspire to leadership positions per se, but are willing to serve when it is evident their level of knowledge or expertise makes them the logical choice to direct others. As leaders, *Is* are low keyed, non-demonstrative, but do have high standards for their team. When they are leading a group of people, *Is* may strike some on their team as being aloof or distant. In addition, *Is* are not confrontational leaders when they need to be. Rather, they expect everyone to be professional, perform at their best and become knowledgeable within their jobs. Thus, *Is* are neither direct providing positive feedback, nor when they must criticize someone's performance. Nevertheless, *Is* are critical by nature, so are apt to more readily spot flaws in other's performance than what they are doing well. In fact, *Is* will take for granted good results and performance, because that is what they expect from others.

*Is* are planners and strategists. Therefore, as leaders they take a long-range view of their area of responsibility. Moreover, they are comfortable working from general goals and direction. *Is* will sort through these and develop plans based upon their assessment of requirements and the organization's overall goals. Unfortunately, *Is* are inclined to spend too much time in the planning process. They will review *many* different scenarios, factors and information before moving into action. In this sense, *Is* are not expeditious, but need to become more so. In any case, once plans are finalized, *Is* establish roles for team members based upon a review of their skills, knowledge and expertise. *Is* are steady, not fast, in progressing toward their goals.

*I*-leaders are vigilant. That is, they pay attention to details and closely monitor processes at all times. They insist members of their team do so as well. However, they are not always as attuned to practical business issues as they should be. *Is* may be unwilling to compromise quality, for example. Even when relaxing their standards somewhat would not hurt end results significantly, but *would* enhance the bottom line.

As indicated earlier, *Is* can fail to pay enough attention to the people side of leading and motivating others. Their natural inclination is to avoid this side of their leadership responsibilities because they are not people or relationship oriented. Yet, *Is* are fair, generally do not play favorites, nor do they throw their weight around and abuse their authority.

As leaders, *Is* do try to foster learning. They will teach those who show an interest in developing a higher level of skill within their jobs. As teachers, they can be patient with such individuals. However, they are not patient with people who only exhibit a limited or half-hearted interest in the work they perform. When instructing, *Is* must be careful to speak and teach at the level of their "audience." As it is, *Is* can tend to talk "above other's heads," usually unintentionally. Beyond this, *I*-leaders are good resources when others on the team have work-related problems.

## Interests: occupational and academic

*Is* prefer activities—on and off the job—that allow them to use their minds, require thought, development of skills and some intelligence to master. *Is* are not particularly action-oriented so participating in sporting events may be uninteresting for them—unless, they become intrigued with the strategy involved. It is not surprising, then, that many *Is* find the game of chess fascinating. For *Is*, hobbies can be extensions of work-related activities or utilize many of the same skills. Thus, a chemist may enjoy experimenting with different combinations of nutrients in feeding their garden.

## Occupational

In general, *Is* seek higher education that will allow them to pursue technical, scientific, and analytically-oriented occupations. Such academic areas as physics, computer science, psychology, astronomy, and statistics would be natural fits for *Is*. Furthermore, *Is* can be ambitious, but not in the usual sense. Their ambitions and aspirations revolve around learning and using their minds to their full potential. Mastering a body of knowledge and adding it to what is known in their chosen field can be important to *Is*.

## Academic

*Is* are often academically-oriented in high school. Many enjoy advanced math, the sciences, computer classes and the like. In fact, *Is* seek higher education and advanced degrees more readily (and more often) than the other themes. They normally pursue courses of study in high school that are intended for college-bound students. Because *Is* are independent and enjoy learning, they usually have the necessary self-discipline to succeed in college. Yet, they may not fair well in all courses. Required courses that are not affiliated with their majors may prove to be uninteresting—particularly for *Is* who are narrowly focused on exactly what they want to major in during their college studies. Classes in marketing and business, in general, will not appeal to most *Is*. The exception would be courses with an analytic element, such as economics or marketing research.

## College programs that fall within the Investigative theme:

Aeronautical Engineering
Anesthesiology
Anthropology
Archaeology
Astronomy
Biochemistry
Biology
Biomedical Engineering
Botany
Business Systems Analyst
Chemical Engineering
Chemistry
Civil Engineering
Cognitive Psychology
Computer Engineering
Computer Programming
Criminology
Dentistry
Dermatology

Developmental Psychology
Ecology
Economics
Electronic Technology
Endocrinology
Epidemiology
Fire Control Technology
Fisheries Science
Genetics
Geography
Geology
Geophysics
Health Sciences
Horticulture
Immunology
Industrial Technology
Internal Medicine
Laser Technology
Marine Biology
Mathematics
Medical Technology
Metallurgy
Microbiology

Mycology
Natural Sciences
Neurology
Nuclear Engineering
Nuclear Physics
Obstetrics / Gynecology
Optometry
Paleontology
Pharmacy
Physics
Physiology
Psychiatry
Psychology
Psychopharmacology
Radiology
Sociology
Statistics
Textile Science
Toxicology
Urology
Veterinary Medicine
X-ray Technology
Zoology

**Self-test**

The following questionnaire is designed to help you determine how closely you match up with the Investigative Holland theme. You will be asked to check-off ("√") answers you think describe yourself or match your interests. *Do not be surprised if you √ many or only a few phrases or words on this questionnaire.* For each section, honestly respond to the questions. Do not hurry. Move at a comfortable, relaxed pace.

<u>Part 1</u> Directions: Indicate with a √ which of the following phrases describe you on the job or come close to your views.

\_      I am systematic when approaching projects or assignments.

\_      I evaluate all options and their pros/cons before deciding.

\_      I want to know the hows and whys when tackling new assignments.

\_      I am regarded as a sound resource for others needing technical advice or information at work.

\_      I can be too rational and tend to discount "soft" or emotional data when making decisions.

\_      Managers should be selected based upon the depth of their knowledge about a department's operations..

\_      I am comfortable handling conceptual, theoretical or abstract problems.

\_      I have considerable intellectual curiosity compared to most people I have worked with before.

<u>Part 2</u>  Directions: From the list of words or phrases below, indicate with a √ those that are *descriptive of you.*

__ reserved        __ curious        __ logical        __ methodical

__ philosophical    __ critical        __ too deliberate    __ enjoy complexity

__ conceptual       __ enjoy research   __ introspective    __ distrust intuition

<u>Part 3</u>  Directions: From the list of Occupations and College Majors below, indicate those you think you would enjoy or find interesting with a √. *Do not worry if you lack the expertise or education to excel in these areas.*

__ Biologist          __ Lab Technician       __ Chemical Engineer

__ Anthropologist    __ Technical Writer     __ Optometrist

__ Astronomy        __ Behavioral Sciences    __ Electronic Technology

__ Statistics         __ Pharmacy          __ Systems Analysis

<u>Directions for scoring:</u> Add all of the √s you made in each of the three parts. The total number of √s is your score on the Investigative Holland theme. Enter that total score below.

My raw score on the Investigative theme is: _____ (Enter your total score)

This score falls within the _____ percentile range (Refer to chapter 7)

This score falls within the _____ category (Refer to chapter 7)

## Developmental advice

If your score on the "self-test" was in the *high* or *average* ranges, you may find some of the suggestions that follow helpful.

If you choose to work on any of these areas, do not attempt to do too much at once. Select *two* or *three* items. Enlist the support and encouragement of persons you respect in this process and seek their feedback and advice periodically.

1) Your tendency to be reserved can come across as aloofness or arrogance. Open up more on a personal level to people at work. Be less formal and become more *informal* and casual on the job.

2) When communicating information, gage the knowledge level and familiarity of your "audience" with the topic. Speak and explain things at *their* level. Do not over-explain.

3) Enhance your level of decisiveness. Avoid over-analyzing problems, doing more research than necessary, or holding off making decisions too long.

4) Expedite your work and projects. Do only as much planning and strategizing as is truly needed. Avoid being overly methodical and too thorough. Do not exceed quality standards.

5) When making decisions and planning, take account of practical matters and do not over-engineer solutions. Ensure decisions can be justified based on business considerations.

6) Become more venturesome. Explore areas of your job where risk taking would not only be justified, but could lead to significant gains. Think beyond the norm.

7) Become more assertive. Be willing to state your views even if you are not 100% sure of yourself. Be more insistent to insure your needs are met and your voice is heard.

8) As a supervisor, be quick to give credit or praise, and be straightforward and direct when criticism is warranted. Do not hold off disciplining employees if it is justified.

9) Become better attuned to the people side of your job. Build bridges to people in different areas of the organization. Be alert to the needs, feelings and concerns of your employees.

10) When working on particularly intriguing or challenging problems or projects, avoid devoting more time to them than is necessary.

11) As a leader, avoid setting your standards for other's performance too high. Involve your team and others in the process of establishing goals, standards and expectations.

12) Learn about how to motivate different types of people. Seek out relevant books, seminars, coworkers, et cetera.

## Final comment

If your score on the self-test was in the *high* range, you may need to broaden your interests and become accepting of people who are different from yourself. People characterized by the Enterprising theme would be most different from you in interests, personality and values. Re-read chapter 5 to learn about such people and their interests.

# CHAPTER 3

◆

# ARTISTIC TYPES:
## "WE LIKE CREATING."

As indicated in the title of this chapter, Artistic types (*As*) of people like "creating." This is as opposed to their preferring things, conceptual ideas, interacting with a lot of different people, leading others or being concerned with order, efficiency and manipulating data. If given a choice, *As* would prefer to deal with other people who have a similar preference. This is not to say *As* are unable or unwilling to do other things or interact with other types of people. They can, of course. However, they like to stick with their preferences if at all possible. Yet, *As* interests and preferences can take on a variety of forms. So too, can their abilities. Their personalities are also broader than might be inferred by the above comments. Let's take a look at what makes an *A* an *A*.

## Interpersonal style

The manner in which *As* relate to others can vary considerably. Some are quite sociable, outgoing and amiable. Others can be much the opposite; quiet, shy, and uncomfortable dealing with people. The underlying issue here, may have much to do with confidence. That is, artistic or creative people often have to, or do, struggle with the need for their work or ideas to be accepted by others. Those who are self-assured are apt to be more extraverted; all other things being equal. Yet, this attribute can change over time—in the direction of a higher degree of extraversion—provided their work and ideas are, indeed, accepted and applauded. Beyond this, *As* will be affected noticeably in this regard by their second-highest Holland theme. For example, if an *A's* second-highest theme is *S* or *E*, they will be more outgoing than if their second highest theme is *R, I* or *C*. The *S* or *E* component will "encourage" extroverted behavior because these two themes are the most outgoing of all, while the *R, I* and *C* themes are reserved, guarded or introverted.

Generally, *As* are interesting people, whether they are open with others or not. This flows from the fact that they are "idea people." They often see the world, problems and many other things (even the mundane) in fresh, new ways. This quality can help spur others' thinking and "free them" of mental chains that could limit their perspectives. Thus, *As* can be valuable in innovative organizations that must change and be creative to stay ahead of the competition. These same qualities will make the *A*-type a misfit in conservative, cautious organizations. If *As* find themselves in such environments, they can experience considerable anxiety and tension while feeling constricted. Not surprisingly, *As* in such organizations are apt to have few friends, feel like they are an outsider and, probably, not stay for long—hopefully, for their own sake.

The emotionalism of the *As* can cause them to be viewed by others as moody or excitable. This reflects the fact that there can be unevenness—more so than other types—in terms of their temperament. Furthermore, when *As* become discouraged, it can be to an extreme degree. Some may become depressed or withdraw from interaction with others.

## Talents, abilities and decision making

The abilities of *As* tend to be diverse, but are characterized by being creative and imaginative. The expression of these abilities can take many forms and would include composing music, drawing/painting, writing and acting/dancing abilities.

*As* are often original thinkers, capable of generating ideas that are new and innovative. They are able to see problems and issues from a unique perspective as a result of their open-minded outlook. Usually, *As* are comfortable dealing with ambiguous, loosely-defined problems and can be strong, conceptual thinkers. Moreover, they are instinctive and can make effective decisions using their intuition. What is more, *As* typically have a refined aesthetic sense. This is the ability to effectively determine examples of appealing or sound design, composition or art.

*As* whose skills lie in the area of writing, will be strong in their verbal ability and have a broad vocabulary. Those who are musically inclined find expression as singers, composers, musicians, and demonstrate an ability to discriminate sounds, tones and rhythms. Visual artists are strong with respect to their spatial and perceptual skills (ability to differentiate fine details). Many possess strong "visual" memory, that is, an ability to mentally store and later recall (in vivid detail) a scene, picture, et cetera. Some visual artists possess exceptional hand-eye coordination, excellent fine motor skills (ability to physically manipulate small objects), as well as mechanical ability (e.g., architects). Those whose artistic side emerges through acting/dancing demonstrate strong emotive skills and an ability to translate words into physical and verbal expressions of emotions. Possession of acting skills can result in *As* being persuasive and having sales ability. Such *As* are likely to be effective oral communicators.

*As* often learn most readily in situations where they are inspired and encouraged to be flexible, and when there is a good deal of variety and stimulation of their senses. *As* are weaker with respect to their analytical and logical thinking abilities (they're prone to rely on their instincts versus their minds). They may also have difficulty with concrete or practical issues/problems, as they can be rather idealistic and overlook common sense considerations. Related to this, *As* emotions can cloud their objectivity and ability to think rationally or realistically. Some may not be adept written or oral communicators.

As suggested earlier, if the *A's* creativity falls in the realm of verbal proficiency, they can be effective selling their ideas to others. Thus, they can weave arguments in a compelling fashion, being dramatic and emotional in order to win others to their cause. There is a danger here, however. Note that *As* are more instinctive than analytical or logical thinkers. Combine this with effective persuasive skills and you have someone, (potentially) who can compel others to make important decisions on the basis of intuition that may or may not rest on sound, objective footing. In essence, it may be best to rely upon the better judgement and analytical skills of other types to decide if the ideas of *As* are truly viable.

The above indicates *As* do allow subjective factors and feelings to override their objectivity. As well, they can be too quick to arrive at a conclusion or judgement. In this regard, *As* formulate opinions without probing into the depths of a problem or issue. Consequently, some of their decisions may represent effective short term or interim measures versus long-term solutions.

## Work style and motivational factors

*As* are most comfortable in work settings that allow them freedom from sharp criticism while offering acceptance and openness to innovative thinking. They can be tireless workers when handling projects or assignments that pique their imagination and interest. In fact, it is not unusual for *As,* in such situations, to lose track of time as they become totally immersed in what they are doing. However, many *As* are likely to be less effective—and less creative—when operating in structured, non-flexible environments. In these types of environments, they will surely feel stifled and frustrated.

When inspired, *As* are not easily daunted by obstacles and can be extremely resourceful working through or around them. They also need variety in their work and quickly become bored with routine, repetitive tasks or responsibilities. And, while *As* can be impressive in their attention to detail in areas that capture their interest, they can be very *inconsistent* in this regard. Many *As* would benefit from time management and priority-setting assistance. This is due to their tendency to lose track of time and focus too much on things they enjoy.

Not surprisingly, *As* are motivated by the chance to express themselves and their creativity. They also have a need for recognition and acceptance from others at work. Such things as money, power, prestige, control, achievement are secondary, at best, when it comes to motivating them. A strong need for nurturance is also important to *As* because they do need encouragement and support from others to excel in some situations. Given that the expression of creativity usually requires an open, flexible environment, *As* also need room for autonomy and independence.

In organizations, *As* can be a "breath of fresh air" who bring a whole new perspective to problems or other matters others may have overlooked or been unable to see.

## Leadership

The leadership style of *As* can vary the most compared to the other themes. This is due to several reasons. One, *As* can be either introverted or extroverted or vary along this dimension from time to time or across situations. Two, *As* can be quite verbally expressive or not particularly so. Three, *As* are emotionally sensitive. Their emotions can determine how outgoing or expressive they are at a given point in time. Four, depending upon the people with whom they are interacting, *As* can be more or less at ease with them.

The above having been said, a few conclusions can be reached about *As* leadership style. They can show great passion for goals they and their team are working toward. When this occurs, their enthusiasm will come through whether they are highly expressive or not. The *As* enthusiasm, in turn, can have a positive and motivating effect on their team. Furthermore, *As* can generate energy in others through their own strong sense of anticipation.

As leaders, *As* can also negatively affect their team if they are only tepid about a goal or project. Then, neither can *As* feign enthusiasm nor hide their *lack* of it.

The above indicates that *As* who lead, may exhibit an ability to transfer their feelings and emotions directly onto their team—for better *and* worse. On the downside, this can result in inconsistent direction across time. Coupled with this, is the fact *As* pour most of their energy into things they find most enjoyable, and commensurately less into things they do not like. Members of an *A*-leader's team will take this cue and may focus most of *their* attention on tasks they find enjoyable as well. As a result, some priorities of the *A*-leader's team may not receive as much attention as they should. This can occur whether or not the *A*-leader has been clear and specific conveying their priorities to the team. Essentially, the actions *not the words* of the *A*-leader may have greater influence in this regard.

*As* often make the workplace enjoyable and fun. They see no reason not to. They hate uninspired routines and will not encumber themselves nor their team with these. This means *As* will occasionally skirt organizational rules, protocol or procedures. They may do this, in some cases, because they have become bored and want to stir things up a bit. Obviously, this can be frustrating to people who value and do follow rules and procedures or the chain of command. This can certainly place *A*-leaders at odds with others in the organization.

Oftentimes, *As* are rather spontaneous. This translates into their being quick to share positive feedback or an encouraging word with members of their team. It also translates into their being equally quick to say what they do not like about other people and their work. However, since *As* can often be just as open with praise *and* criticism, people tend to accept each from them once they know the *As* style.

*A*-leaders do not shy away from tackling huge projects that, perhaps, others have avoided. If it is interesting, *As* are up to the challenge. *As* can bring a sweeping sense of vision to projects they manage. They will tend to jump right in and get started, not necessarily with much of a plan. Instead, *As* are willing to trust their instincts and resourcefulness to get things accomplished. Unfortunately, this can certainly result in their heading down the wrong path at times then, having to backtrack later. In this sense, *As* are action-oriented leaders who prefer to have many different things going on at once. This brings up another potential shortcoming of *As*: they can run into trouble staying organized and may lose track of details.

Yet, somehow, some way, *As* do manage to pull things together—often at the last minute—to reach goals and deadlines.

### Interests: occupational and academic

*As* prefer activities that allow them to use their acquired skills in creative ways. Producing artwork, crafts, sculpture, music or poetry are a few areas of interest to them. They are also keenly interested in refining and expanding their artistic or creative abilities. Moreover, *As* will readily explore ways in which to apply what they know in new areas. They can have wide-ranging interests, reflecting their venturesome outlook and instinctive curiosity.

### <u>Occupational</u>

*As* may or may not pursue higher education in the fields of music, writing, fine arts, theater or other areas. Whether they do or not, is often dependent upon the confidence they have in their skills *and* the amount of encouragement they have received from important people in their lives. Some *As* may not pursue formal art education per se, because of the dearth of art-oriented occupations and careers that exist. So, they may pursue a secondary interest in college and keep their artistic interests and skills alive through other means. Many *As* hold down jobs in non-art fields (which could be related to other Holland themes), and pursue their artistic interests in off-work hours. Occupations *As* can and do pursue include art or music teacher, graphic artist, actor, musician, illustrator, architect, playwright, police sketch artist, or art director.

## Academic

*As* academic interests are generally non-technical and non-scientific. Business-related courses would hold little appeal for them, and neither would any course requiring rote memorization. As a general rule, *As* do not enjoy courses that are rigidly structured. Nevertheless, they may take to scientific or other courses if (an important "if"), the instructor teaches in an imaginative or creative way. And, surprisingly, while most *As* express an aversion to math courses, many report having enjoyed—even done well in—geometry. Bear in mind, geometry has a strong visual component that aligns with certain abilities displayed by *As*. Of course, *As* primary interest is creativity and any course that is artistically oriented. Depending upon their creative orientation, *As* may prefer creative writing classes, music and composition or drawing, painting and sculpture, in addition to dance, drama and theater. For some, their interests could include marketing and advertising courses. Biology, as it relates to anatomy and anatomy, can also capture the interest of some *As*. *As* certainly prefer colleges dedicated to artistic orientations to hone their creative skills. If *As* have doubts about their skill level, they may apply to an art program within a larger college or university, instead of a college dedicated solely to their field of art, music or drama.

## College programs that fall within the Artistic theme:

Arabic
Architecture
Archival Science
Art (and Music)
Therapy
Art Education
Art History and
Appreciation
Arts Management
Asiatic Languages
Auctioneering
Audiology
Biblical Languages
Ceramics
Chinese
Cinematography
and Film
Classics
Commercial Art
Commercial Pho-
tography
Composition
Crafts
Creative Writing
Dance
Dance Therapy

Dramatic Arts and
Theater
Drawing
English
English Education
Fashion Merch-
andising
Fiber / Textiles /
Weaving
Film Animation
Film Arts
Fine Arts
Foreign Language
Education
French
German
Greek
Hebrew
Home Decorating
Industrial Design
Interior Design
Intermedia
Italian
Japanese
Landscape Archi-
tecture
Literature

Literature, American
Literature, Com-
parative
Medical Illustrating
Metalworking /
Jewelry
Music Education
Music Performance
Music Theory and
Composition
Native American
Languages
Painting
Photography
Printmaking
Radio and Television
Rehabilitation Ser-
vices
Religious Music
Rhetoric
Social Psychology
Speech, Debate
and Forensics
Theater Design
Visual & Performing
Arts

## Self-test

The following questionnaire is designed to help you determine how closely you match up with the Artistic Holland theme. You will be asked to check-off ("√") answers you think describe yourself or match your interests. *Do not be surprised if you √ many or only a few phrases or words on this questionnaire.* For each section, honestly respond to the questions. Do not hurry. Move at a comfortable, relaxed pace.

<u>Part 1</u> Directions: Indicate with a √ which of the following phrases describe you on the job or come close to your views.

____ I prefer to have many different assignments, responsibilities.

____ I am quite flexible in the use of guidelines.

____ I am not afraid to try or suggest new ideas, approaches.

____ I operate best when following my inspirations.

____ I sometimes become scattered or unfocused.

____ Managers should embrace radical or innovative changes in work methods, systems or procedures to keep workers motivated.

____ When necessary, I can produce many novel ideas.

____ Some people think I am unusual, or that I see things very differently from others.

<u>Part 2</u>  Directions: From the list of words or phrases below, indicate with a √ those that are *descriptive of you.*

_ original          _ open          _ imaginative   _ expressive

_ spontaneous    _ temperamental  _ impulsive     _ disorganized

_ unconventional  _ fun-loving      _ fresh outlook  _ flexible thinker

<u>Part 3</u>  Directions: From the list of Occupations and College Majors below, indicate those you think you would enjoy or find interesting with a √. *Do not worry if you lack the expertise or education to excel in these areas.*

_ Commercial Designer   _ Composer        _Sculptor

_ Set Designer           _ Painter          _Drama Teacher

_ Architecture           _ Graphic Arts     _ Interior Design

_ Literature             _ Art History      _Medical Illustrating

<u>Directions for scoring:</u> Add all of the √s you made in each of the three parts. The total number of √s is your score on the Artistic Holland theme. Enter that total score below.

My raw score on the Artistic theme is: _____ (Enter your total score)

This score falls within the _____ percentile range (Refer to chapter 7)

This score falls within the _____ category (Refer to chapter 7)

## Developmental advice

If your score on the "self-test" was in the *high* or *average* ranges, you may find some of the suggestions that follow helpful.

If you choose to work on any of these areas, do not attempt to do too much at once. Select *two* or *three* items. Enlist the support and encouragement of persons you respect in this process and seek their feedback and advice periodically.

1) You may benefit from exploring ways to boost your confidence. Be sure to give yourself credit for your accomplishments, things you do well and the skills you have developed. Do not look too much to others for affirmation of your value or worth.

2) Try to reign in some of your stronger feelings and emotions so they do not interfere with your ability to relate effectively to others.

3) Be sure to consider the practical implications of some of your creative or innovative ideas. Weigh the downside as carefully as you allow yourself to become excited about the upside.

4) For the benefit of *others*, be sure to organize projects you manage. Share important information with your team, and do not shift goals and priorities too often and without good reason.

5) Do not neglect uninteresting, boring, routine or repetitive aspects of your job. Discipline yourself to make sure these areas are given proper attention.

6) Avoid overselling the benefits of your ideas to others. Have someone whose opinion you trust, review your ideas to catch any flaws or oversights.

7) Be careful making significant decisions when you are excited, angry, frustrated, feeling very up *or* down. Be aware of personal, subjective factors that could unduly influence your decisions.

8) Always consider the long-term ramifications of decisions. Do not focus too much on the here and now.

9)     Accept that organizations have rules, policies, protocols and pro-
       cedures. Do not skirt these if it will cause frustration, hardship,
       difficulty, or extra work for others.

10)    As a leader, provide clear goals, standards and expectations for
       your team. Be sure you establish clear lines of accountability for
       everyone.

11)    Be sure you and your team are not so caught up having fun, that
       any aspect of the work is overlooked.

12)    Do not bite off more than you can chew. That is, do not tackle
       larger projects than you, and those you must depend upon, can
       truly handle. Evaluate available resources and your team carefully.

## Final comment

If your score on the self-test was in the *high* range, you may need to
broaden your interests and become accepting of people who are different
from yourself. People characterized by the Conventional theme would be
most different from you in interests, personality and values. Re-read chapter 6 to learn about such people and their interests.

# CHAPTER 4

◆

# SOCIAL TYPES: "WE LIKE HELPING."

As indicated in the title of this chapter, Social types (*Ss*) of people like "helping." This is as opposed to their preferring things, conceptualizing ideas, being creative, leading others or being concerned with order, efficiency and manipulating data. If given a choice, *Ss* would prefer to deal with other people who have a similar preference. This is not to say *Ss* are unable or unwilling to do other things or interact with other types of people. They can, of course. However, they like to stick with their preferences if at all possible. Yet, *Ss* interests and preferences can take on a variety of forms. So too, can their abilities. Their personalities are also broader than might be inferred by the above comments. Let's take a look at what makes an *S* an *S*.

## Interpersonal style

Interpersonally, *Ss* are warm, considerate and caring. They extend themselves readily to others and make a conscious effort to put people at ease in their presence. Thus, they are comfortable to be around and approachable. If *Rs* and *Cs* are dependable, task-focused foundations upon which to build a team, *Ss* are the comforting, people-oriented cement that holds others together in a work environment.

The helpful nature of *Ss* make them ideal candidates for any service-providing role. They not only enjoy meeting others' needs, they excel at being able to do so. In this regard, their non-aggressive style and willingness to listen actively to others are solid assets. The danger for *Ss* is their easygoing, helpful and responsive nature can be taken advantage of by those who are manipulative or shrewd. Likewise, *Ss* can be too generous with their time. In addition, the trustfulness of the *Ss* can work against them (they can be naïve, and too idealistic). In fact, *Ss* may need to become more questioning of others' intentions and motives, instead of simply taking people at their word or face value.

The emotional sensitivity and empathy of *Ss* can work for *and* against them. These attributes work for them by allowing *Ss* to readily get along with people. They work against *Ss* in a few ways. One, *Ss* can be overly sympathetic—to the point where they place their own needs and feelings second. Two, when others let them down, or do not live up to promises, *Ss* can be too forgiving and willing to offer a second (or third) chance to those who are undeserving. Three, *Ss* can take negative or seemingly negative comments too personally and to heart. Four, they are prone to take interpersonal setbacks hard and be slow to rebound.

Since *Ss* are largely "people-pleasers," they are not assertive individuals. Thus, their needs, feelings, accomplishments, ideas, et cetera, can be overlooked. *Ss* would benefit by being willing to press for their needs and prepared to "sing their own praises" now and then, to be sure they receive the recognition, support, and opportunities they deserve.

It should be noted that *Ss* are non-confrontational and prefer to side-step or avoid conflict, disagreements and other unpleasant interpersonal situations. Their natural inclination is to maintain harmony. Considering this, *Ss* can compromise too readily or sacrifice their needs and interests to avoid confrontations. Consequently, they may settle for less than what they want, need, deserve or expect.

## Talents, abilities and decision making

The abilities of this type generally fall within the realm of working with people, rather than things or ideas. *Ss* have strong human relations skills, and often do well in roles where they must work in a team setting. They are capable of drawing good ideas out of others because they are encouraging and supportive. *Ss* are also generous offering their time to others.

In a broader sense, *Ss* possess effective facilitative skills. They are capable of bringing people together to work cooperatively while achieving their goals. Along with this, *Ss* are skilled at resolving conflicts among other people when disputes arise. In this regard, *Ss* are adept at "smoothing over" differences, and finding a compromise acceptable to the parties involved.

Many *Ss* have strong verbal, written and oral skills. Thus, they often communicate effectively and are attentive listeners. These qualities make *Ss* adept when it comes to understanding and resolving people problems. Beyond this, *Ss* are emotionally expressive, which is a sound asset when they are trying to persuade or influence others to support their ideas. *Ss* usually learn best in socially interactive settings where they are able to openly discuss their views, and there is much encouragement for doing so.

*Ss* are usually weaker with respect to their physical, spatial and mechanical abilities. And, while they can be intelligent, *Ss* may not be impressive with respect to their logical or critical thinking abilities, (their feelings, sensitivity and emotions can interfere.) Likewise, *Ss* may have difficulty with theoretical problems or issues that are scientific in nature. In a different vein, while *Ss* are generally supportive of their organization's goals, they are not particularly business minded. This means some of their decisions may not make complete sense from a strictly business point of view. In addition, *Ss* are not as effective in settings where they must work alone or with a high degree of autonomy because they receive strength from working with and around other people.

## Work style and motivational factors

On the job, *Ss* respect the needs of others and can effectively coordinate their efforts to achieve established goals. They also want to do what is right by others and enjoy working in a team-oriented, collegial environment. *Ss* are apt to be careful completing their work because they do not want to let others down, or make more work for coworkers. In this sense, they are most likely to err on the side of being too detailed when completing assignments than less so. This indicates, however, that *Ss* are not risk takers, which is true. They are especially likely to play it safe when decisions they make might negatively effect those around them.

*Ss* are neither exceptionally strategic nor highly tactical when going about their jobs. While they do consider some of the long-range ramifications of their actions or plans, their ability to think *many* steps ahead, adeptly establish priorities, and manage their time is not as strong as their people skills. This probably reflects the fact *Ss* have chosen to hone their interpersonal skills over these skills. Yet, *Ss* are certainly careful about meeting important daily or short term demands. In addition, *Ss* can actually be skilled at visualizing the long-term consequences of decisions *on people*, especially when the results are likely to be negative.

*Ss* are motivated by strong social needs on the job. They *need* to be around people, and find being alone frustrating, unpleasant or uncomfortable. *Ss* also have a strong need to feel valued, appreciated and respected. In addition, *Ss* appreciate and look forward to being recognized by others for their "good deeds," not so much for the recognition per se, as for the acknowledgement that what they are doing is, indeed, valued by others.

*Ss* are not particularly ambitious—at least not in the usual sense of the word. Their desire to move up in an organization is likely to have much to do with altruistic motives. That is, *Ss* are likely to believe they can do more positive things for others in a higher level position, than in one lower on the organizational chart.

Considering their strong social and affiliation needs, *Ss* are not particularly interested in operating with a high degree of autonomy and independence. Yet, the strong social requirements of *Ss* can cause them to indulge this need too much at times. As a result, *Ss* can socialize too much on the job, and can be too chatty or talkative during conversations or meetings.

## Leadership

*Ss* do aspire to *serve* others in a leadership role—for altruistic reasons rather than those related to control and power. If asked to serve others in this way, *Ss* will feel honored to do so. They take such responsibilities seriously and want to do the right thing by the people under their direction.

The leadership style of *Ss* is nurturing, facilitative and participative. They are warmly enthusiastic as well. *S*-leaders freely involve team members in goal setting, planning and decision making. *Ss* also strive to create a caring, supportive environment that rewards cooperation. They are best suited to directing teams that are focused on delivering a service, but not in an extremely competitive, aggressive, impersonal organization.

*Ss* must take care not to be too relaxed and easygoing as leaders, nor insufficiently demanding of others. As it is, they are inclined to keep demands relatively light, while leading with a "soft touch." This means *Ss* may not always get the best performance out of each individual team member. For example, those who need new challenges, a "push" or "room to operate independently," may fail to reach their full potential under an S-leader.

People reporting to Ss will notice they are quick to offer a pat on the back, a "thank you," or other forms of positive feedback. On the other hand, Ss avoid being critical, even when such feedback is warranted, justified and necessary. They simply find it unpleasant to confront others. Unfortunately, Ss can find their easygoing management style taken advantage of and their patience and authority tested by some people. Consequently, some personnel problems can snowball and worsen to the point where Ss are finally forced to take action. In particular, Ss do everything they can to salvage a poorly performing employee, which is admirable; however, terminating such an individual may actually be in the best interest (in the long run) of all parties involved.

As leaders, Ss follow established rules and procedures most of the time. When they do not, it is usually due to their interpreting policies as unfair to their employees. Furthermore, Ss are cautious decision makers who are not inclined to take risks. This is certainly true if they feel someone could or might be hurt as a result of doing so. The downside to this propensity is that Ss can inadvertently discourage members of their team from being venturesome and can miss opportunities as a result.

Ss often develop close ties with people they lead. They take a personal interest in each team member, are attentive to remembering such things as employee's birthdays, likes/dislikes, and try to make everyone feel special, valued and appreciated. Ss do have to be careful about crossing the line between being a "friendly manager," and a *friend* to those they lead. Occasionally, Ss may blur the line of distinction between their role as leader, and that of "friend," with those under their direction. This can weaken their objectivity when they must assess their employee's performance. S-managers must also be careful about being too protective of their team. They sometimes become defensive if "outsiders" criticize anyone they supervise.

In many cases, *Ss* do a fine job in a training or instructional role. In these roles, they are patient, understanding and empathetic. *Ss* often demonstrate a seemingly, innate ability to relate well to a wide range of people, and meet them at their level of understanding. Not surprisingly, *Ss* can be fine mentors and find such roles gratifying and fulfilling.

## Interests: occupational and academic

*Ss* prefer activities involving other people. Their interests typically include those that allow them to help or assist others in some way. Volunteering would be one broad category of interest for *Ss*. Getting together with family and friends would also occupy a good deal of their non-work time. On the other hand, *Ss* tend to avoid highly competitive pursuits, as these are inimical to their core values of service and cooperation. This does not mean *Ss* avoid sports participation. On the contrary, they enjoy such activities—for the chance they provide to interact with other people. Hobbies *Ss* would choose tend not to be solitary—unless, the product of the hobby was to be given to someone. Instead, they enjoy organizing and participating in group activities, and are often active in charitable work such as fund-raising. Golf is a notable *S*-theme leisure interest.

## <u>Occupational</u>

The career and occupational interests of *Ss* normally have a "helping" or "giving" component to them. Such areas as nursing, social work, teaching, human resource management, physical therapy and food services, would be comfortable fits for *Ss*. They have a strong preference for organizations that truly value their employees, and where their contributions are appreciated and recognized. Extremely political, strongly results-oriented, or competitive organizations, would not be good fits for *Ss*.

## Academic

*Ss* are typically conscientious students. In part, this is because they want to please their teachers or instructors by doing well. At the same time, *Ss* do have an interest in academic coursework and many go on to pursue higher education. *Ss* have a natural affinity for the social sciences, teaching, and different types of counseling, but typically show little interest in technical, scientific studies. *Ss* can also show an interest in areas of business education that focus on serving people. *Ss* learn readily in interactive group settings where information and ideas are freely exchanged. They often enjoy studying together with fellow students. One thing *Ss* must be careful about, as students, is to ensure they focus sufficient time on actual studying and avoid too much on socializing.

# College programs that fall within the Social theme:

Adult & Continuing Education

Agricultural Services

Athletic Training

Bartending

Bible Studies

Child Care Management

Clinical Psychology

Community Services

Corrections

Cosmetology

Counseling Psychology

Criminal Justice

Dental Assisting

Driver Education

Education

Educational Administration

Family Services

Food and Nutrition

Foster Care

Geriatrics

Health Education

History

Home Economics

Home Health Aide

Industrial / Organizational Psychology

Law Enforcement

Legal Assisting

Library Science

Medical Records Administration

Medical / Surgical Nursing

Mental Health Technology

Missionary Studies

Nursing

Nursing Assisting

Nutritional Sciences

Occupational Therapy

Organizational Behavior

Outdoor Recreation

Peace Studies

Personality Psychology

Physical Education

Physical Therapy

Podiatric Assisting

Preventive Medicine

Public Policy Studies

Radiologic Technology

Recreational Therapy

Rehabilitation Counseling

Religion

Respiratory Therapy Assisting

School Psychology

Sign Language

Social Work

Special Education

Speech Pathology Education

Sports / Physical Education

Surgical Nursing

Teacher Aid

Ward Service Management

Women's Studies

**Self-test**

The following questionnaire is designed to help you determine how closely you match up with the Social Holland theme. You will be asked to check-off ("√") answers you think describe yourself or match your interests. *Do not be surprised if you √ many or only a few phrases or words on this questionnaire.* For each section, honestly respond to the questions. Do not hurry. Move at a comfortable, relaxed pace.

<u>Part 1</u>  Directions: Indicate with a √ which of the following phrases describe you on the job or come close to your views.

\_      I am tolerant when working with others.

\_      I am sure to seek input from coworkers before making decisions.

\_      I try to maintain cooperative relations with coworkers.

\_      I can effectively coordinate projects with coworkers.

\_      I sometimes go too far in an effort to be helpful or considerate.

\_      Getting close to employees on a personal level is an excellent way to get them to work hard for you.

\_      I like most of the people I know at work.

\_      I have been let down by people after going out of my way to help them or by being too trusting.

<u>Part 2</u>  Directions: From the list of words or phrases below, indicate with a √ those that are *descriptive of you.*

_ considerate     _ generous     _ non-confrontational _ receptive

_ tenderhearted _ too trusting _ emotional          _ readily compromise

_ helpful         _ good listener _ caring            _ appreciative

<u>Part 3</u>  Directions: From the list of Occupations and College Majors below, indicate those you think you would enjoy or find interesting with a √. *Do not worry if you lack the expertise or education to excel in these areas.*

_ Camp Counselor     _ School Psychologist _ Medical Assistant

_ Athletic Trainer     _ Probation Officer     _ Child Day Care Worker

_ Food & Nutrition     _ Geriatrics             _ Secondary Education

_ Home Economics     _ Clinical Psychology _ Theological Studies

<u>Directions for scoring:</u> Add all of the √s you made in each of the three parts. The total number of √s is your score on the Social Holland theme. Enter that total score below.

My raw score on the Social theme is: _____ (Enter your total score)

This score falls within the _____ percentile range (Refer to chapter 7)

This score falls within the _____ category (Refer to chapter 7)

## Developmental advice

If your score on the "self-test" was in the *high* or *average* ranges, you may find some of the suggestions that follow helpful.

If you choose to work on any of these areas, do not attempt to do too much at once. Select *two* or *three* items. Enlist the support and encouragement of persons you respect in this process and seek their feedback and advice periodically.

1) Guard against becoming overly dependent upon others for advice, guidance or recognition.

2) Do not allow your easygoing nature and willingness to help, be taken advantage of by others. Become somewhat more questioning of other's motives and intentions.

3) Deal with conflict, confrontations and disagreements openly and directly. Do not put off dealing with such matters. Realize positive results can flow from such openness.

4) Work to develop more assertiveness. Do not be so quick to compromise, acquiesce or settle for less than what you need, require or deserve. Learn to become more insistent and outspoken.

5) Prevent your feelings of sympathy and concern from overriding your ability to be objective about people or people problems. Focus on the facts and less on subjective elements.

6) When leading others, be sure you are equally forthright with criticism as you are with praise. Tackle performance problems promptly, and do not hesitate to take necessary disciplinary action.

7) As a decision maker, become more analytical, logical and rational. Do not allow your personal feelings or emotions to carry too much weight. Take full account of business considerations.

8) If managing others, avoid making associates too dependent upon each other or yourself. Give additional autonomy to those who need it. Encourage risk taking and experimentation.

9) Exhibit a greater willingness to take risks yourself. Avoid playing things too safely or cautiously.

10) Be alert to how much time you spend socializing, networking or just chatting at work. Avoid overdoing it.

11) Do not hold back your opinions simply because you think some-one might disagree with you, object strongly or take offense. You may have a valuable perspective others lack and need to hear.

12) As a leader, be sure to keep an appropriate, professional, personal and emotional distance between yourself and those under your direction.

## Final comment

If your score on the self-test was in the *high* range, you may need to broaden your interests and become accepting of people who are different from yourself. People characterized by the Realistic theme would be most different from you in interests, personality and values. Re-read chapter 1 to learn about such people and their interests.

# Chapter 5

---◆---

# Enterprising Types: "We like influencing."

As indicated in the title of this chapter, Enterprising types (*Es*) of people like "influencing." This is as opposed to their preferring things, conceptual ideas, being creative, interacting with a lot of different people, or being concerned with order, efficiency and manipulating data. If given a choice, *Es* would prefer to deal with other people who have a similar preference. This is not to say *Es* are unable or unwilling to do other things or interact with other types of people. They can, of course. However, they like to stick with their preferences if at all possible. Yet, *Es* interests and preferences can take on a variety of forms. So too, can their abilities. Their personalities are also broader than might be inferred by the above comments. Let's take a look at what makes an *E* an *E*.

## Interpersonal style

*Es* are extraverted in relations with others and freely take the social initiative when meeting people. In social situations, they do not hesitate to introduce themselves, strike up a conversation and say what they think. *Es* are also confident of their ability to interact with and influence people. As well, they are often assertive and forceful. Thus, *Es* will readily push for their views, interests or needs. In this regard, *Es* do not easily accept "No" for an answer, and will fight for what they believe in. On the negative side, this can lead to inflexibility, stubbornness or expecting things to *always* go their way.

*Es* are likely to be seen by others as driven, self-starters who enjoy the limelight of a visible leadership role. While they are extraverted and readily take the social initiative, *Es* are not necessarily friendly individuals. Consequently, they are more likely to have many acquaintances than close friends. In addition, within and outside of their organizations, *Es* are effective networkers. They work hard to build a wide circle of contacts whom they can turn to when they need help, information, support, expertise, et cetera.

*Es* can be rather political in their orientation. That is, they sometimes view people as means to a personally valued end, which can cause others to feel *Es* are manipulative. This can make people somewhat leery of them. Further, the aggressiveness of *Es* can be intimidating to those who are mild-mannered, under-confident or reserved. While this is not necessarily their intent, *it can be* if power, control and influence over others becomes their primary objective. Yet, it must be noted that the "political" *E* can be adept at building coalitions needed to achieve broad-scoped objectives important to organizations. In the end, it comes down to exactly *how* they use this attribute, constructively or otherwise.

## Talents, abilities and decision making

The abilities of this type, like the Social type, generally fall within the realm of working with people rather than with things. The difference is *Es* skills revolve around being able to influence, persuade and direct people toward the achievement of important goals. *Es* are often persuasive and strong in terms of their sales ability. In fact, they are assertive, determined to overcome objections, and can develop convincing arguments for their ideas, needs and interests. *Es* typically are effective oral communicators who are comfortable making presentations in front of groups.

*Es* are competitive people, in fact, the most competitive of the Holland themes. They often are persistent and determined going after any valued goal. Furthermore, *Es* are able to effectively manage stress and pressure that occur without losing sight of objectives or becoming discouraged. In fact, *Es* are not easily daunted or discouraged, and display a strong will to overcome obstacles or difficulties. Some *Es* operate particularly well under adversity and rise to the challenge it presents.

*Es* are proactive handling problems and display a sense of urgency when they occur. Thus, they aim to find answers and solutions as quickly as possible, and have an ability to be decisive. *Es* can and will make tough decisions. Thus, when faced with challenging problems, *Es* are prompt, direct and do not shy away from making difficult choices. They are also confident and willing to take advantage of fleeting opportunities that require fast action on their part. Additionally, *Es* are logical thinkers with an ability to accurately size up facts, and other objective information to arrive at reasonable conclusions. However, the logical thinking ability of *Es* is not typically on par with that of *Is* who are the most logical, analytical of the six types. Furthermore, *Es* ability to think logically, is best suited to a business setting or for resolving business problems.

*Es* are notably weaker when it comes to handling details or routine work. They prefer to focus on the bigger picture or broader issues and concerns and leave the details to others. For this reason, and due to their impatience for results, *Es* will have difficulty handling or effectively resolving problems that require painstaking and in-depth analysis or theoretical or abstract issues. *Es* propensity to follow their gut instincts or act quickly to keep things moving forward can work against them in such matters.

*Es* are independent minded. So much so, they are often unable to subjugate their needs or opinions to those of others. Put in different terms, *Es* can be stubborn, willful or too sure of their own views, ideas, or opinions. Finally, *Es* often view themselves, their accomplishments, and ideas in positive—even glowing—terms. Unfortunately, they can be blind to, or gloss over, their shortcomings

## Work style and motivational factors

*Es* are very persistent going after what they want or need. This attribute, and their tenacity, allow *Es* to deliver impressive results when given an objective that requires them to work through others. Coupled with this, is the potential for *Es* to be well-organized in getting things done. In particular, *Es* focus on aspects of projects (or their jobs) where they know the pay off will be greatest. They are able to convince others of their ideas, supply the enthusiasm and energy to get things started, and can coordinate the necessary people and other resources to get the job done.

*Es* are effective when it comes to applying their intelligence and experience to attain their goals. That is, they put forth the necessary mental effort to develop plans and deliver the results they seek. *Es* ensure their plans and strategies are carried through and that snags or difficulties are addressed promptly. Similarly, *Es* are often strategic thinkers with an ability to understand the overall picture. These attributes allow them to develop forward-looking plans that are action-oriented. Likewise, *Es* are risk takers who are typically venturesome in their outlook with an entrepreneurial style. They can be bold, even daring, in their vision and decisions.

But, the results-minded *E* can focus too much on the overall picture and broader objectives and lose sight of mundane, day-to-day demands. They view these as uninteresting or unproductive activities. The same is true of routine decisions or those that *appear to be routine*—*Es* can be hasty with them. Similarly, the *Es* attention to details can be quite variable—especially those they judge to be unimportant, others' opinions notwithstanding.

Underneath it all, *Es* are ambitious and strongly-career oriented. They are certainly willing to make sacrifices for the success they seek. *Es* are strongly motivated by a need to achieve, and make a significant contribution to their organizations. They value prestige, power, money, and actively seek visible leadership roles. The status of an *Es* position is also important, as are job titles and their position on the organizational chart. *Es* are the most highly motivated (and outwardly so) of all themes when it comes to goal achievement. They are certainly the most purely ambitious.

Yet, the ambition of *Es* is not an altogether positive attribute. They can sometimes focus so much on career success and advancement, that their personal lives and relationships suffer. It is not unusual for *Es* to freely accept the requirement of large corporations to frequently move in order to earn promotions. They are equally willing to put in excessive hours on the job to achieve this objective. This can be disruptive for families who receive what is left of the *Es* time and energy after their work is done. *Es* operating thusly, also run the risk of eventual burn out.

## Leadership

In many ways, when people think of a stereotypical leader—confident, decisive, hard-driving, goal oriented and no-nonsense like—they are conjuring the image of Holland's *E*-type. Of course, this sort of leader only represents *one version* of what a leader can be.

Not surprisingly, *Es* have a strong desire to assume a leadership role in whatever situation they find themselves. If no one else steps forward, *Es* will do so eagerly and without hesitation. Essentially, *Es* are willing and prefer to take charge and provide direction to others. They are certainly comfortable assuming responsibility for managing large projects and groups of people. For *Es*, doing so seems natural. Yet, *Es* need to lead is so strong, they may inappropriately take on such roles in situations where they really *are not* the best qualified to do so. Two factors can come into play here. One, *Es* can exhibit so much outward confidence that they convince others they can do the job, despite having private doubts. Two, others may simply accede to the *Es* preferences or assertiveness.

In managerial roles, *Es* readily convey and enjoin confidence. They are clear about goals and expectations. Regarding the latter, *Es* expect a lot from those they manage. They hold people accountable, and do not accept excuses for non-performance. High-performing individuals will be promoted rapidly by *E*-managers. Weak or marginal performers, on the other hand, will not be tolerated for long. *Es* do not hesitate making difficult personnel decisions. When doing so, they focus on a person's contributions to the bottom-line success of the organization. They are objective and businesslike when making these decisions.

Unfortunately, *Es* lack patience for training people, particularly individuals who have potential, but require nurturing and understanding from them to excel. Consequently, *E*-managers can have talented people fall by the wayside, quit, or be dismissed because of this. *Es* can also make the mistake of hiring their top "lieutenants" in their own image. In essence, they look for people having various *E*-qualities to fill top positions. This can, in an extreme scenario, result in intense and harmful competition that leads to those individuals becoming territorial versus cooperative.

As managers, *Es* are certainly demanding. Unfortunately, *Es* can expect too much and are all too ready to transfer their ambitions and high expectations onto their team. But, if others fail to come through as expected, *Es* are direct expressing their displeasure and frustration. *Es* can also exert too much control over their direct reports if they suspect those individuals are not as competent or self-motivated as themselves. This can stifle initiative, creativity and cause undue frustration and stress for such individuals. In a worst case scenario, *Es* can overwork their staffs, drive them too hard, and have difficulty holding onto people for long.

*Es* can create a compelling vision for their operations or organizations. They are capable of thinking broadly and strategically. Likewise, they consider the overall picture when creating goals and objectives. Equally important, is the fact *Es* have the necessary drive and determination to make their visions become reality. They can be inspiring leaders whose vision and audacity can be motivating for those around them.

*Es* often display an entrepreneurial spirit. Many have started organizations and businesses. They find doing so exciting and energizing. Within organizations, some *Es* operate as entrepreneurs. These individuals show a willingness to take risks others would shy away from. They particularly enjoy the challenge of getting a new enterprise off the ground and making it successful.

### Interests: occupational and academic

*Es* prefer competitive activities. Thus, they find many types of sporting events of interest, and prefer to be a participant versus an observer. *Es* find it difficult to "play" without trying hard to win, and will become angry with partners or teammates who do not put forward their best efforts— even in pick-up games. *Es* also enjoy activities that involve an element of chance such as poker, sports betting or casino gambling. Furthermore, *Es* enjoy activities that allow them to influence and persuade others. This could include part-time real estate sales or holding an elective office in a non-work organization.

### <u>Occupational</u>

Because *Es* are ambitious and pursue influential positions within organizations, higher education is usually a key part of their plans to get there. Business related college programs such as marketing, finance, business management are often pursued by *Es*. Political science and law can also be areas of interest to *Es*. They prefer goal-oriented occupations where they can have significant influence. Many different types of managerial positions are of interest to *Es,* as are executive-level roles. *Es* often pursue sales-related careers (though, not customer service roles). Political careers are also attractive to *Es*.

## Academic

Next to *Is*, *Es* are next in line as far as logical thinking goes among the Holland themes. Whereas the *Is* logical thought processes are technically and scientifically oriented, those of *Es* are business oriented. *Es* want to get ahead, and this often shows up even in high school. Frequently, they pursue leadership roles in school (e.g., sports, student government, and other such activities). They are also highly competitive. So, *Es* want to excel in school, not so much for the pursuit of knowledge, but to finish ahead of the pack and earn recognition and rewards. *Es* learn best when there is a clear goal or purpose served through learning, and information is presented in an organized fashion. Therefore, learning for its own sake does not make sense to *Es*.

*Es* show a strong inclination toward business studies and course work (e.g., management, marketing, sales, communications, advertising, banking and finance), in addition to law, pre-law and political science. Many *Es* pursue higher education, undergraduate and graduate programs. In fact, MBA programs, particularly Executive MBA programs, are well populated with them. *Es* do what they think it will take to get ahead academically with both eyes focused on their careers after college. *Es* may fail to devote as much time on required course work as they do on core classes within their chosen program. For *Es*, it is not unusual to see lower, overall grade point averages with significantly higher grades in their fields of interest.

# College programs that fall within the Enterprising theme:

Administrative Assistant

Advertising

American Studies

Aviation Management

Building Maintenance

Business Administration

Business Education

Chef

City Planning

Communications

Construction

Custom Tailoring

Emergency Medical Technology

Entrepreneurship

Executive Secretarial

Fashion Modeling

Finance

Financial Service Marketing

Food Service

Funeral Services

General Marketing

Health Care Administration

Higher Education Administration

Hotel Management

Human Resource Development

Industrial Engineering

Industrial Sales

Information Science and Systems

Insurance and Risk Management

Investments and Securities

Journalism

Junior High Education

Labor / Industrial Relations

Law

Law Enforcement Administration

Management Banking and Finance

Marina Operations

Marketing and Distribution

Marketing Management

Merchant Marine Officer

Personnel Management

Product Management

Property Management

Public Administration

Public Relations

Public Utilities

Purchasing

Real Estate

Restaurant Management

Retailing

Sales

Sports Administration

Travel

Urban Studies

Wholesaling

## Self-test

The following questionnaire is designed to help you determine how closely you match up with the Enterprising Holland theme. You will be asked to check-off ("√") answers you think describe yourself or match your interests. *Do not be surprised if you √ many or only a few phrases or words on this questionnaire.* For each section, honestly respond to the questions. Do not hurry. Move at a comfortable, relaxed pace.

Part 1 Directions: Indicate with a √ which of the following phrases describe you on the job or come close to your views.

\_\_\_  Keep long-range goals clearly in mind at all times.

\_\_\_  Display a keen sense of urgency.

\_\_\_  Display drive, determination and a bias toward action.

\_\_\_  Enjoy taking charge of projects.

\_\_\_  Expect too much, too soon from others.

\_\_\_  Management should push people to their limits to find their true potential and achieve impressive results.

\_\_\_  I do not shy away from taking credit for my accomplishments.

\_\_\_  I am comfortable making presentations or giving an unrehearsed speech.

<u>Part 2</u> Directions: From the list of words or phrases below, indicate with a √ those that are *descriptive of you.*

__ adventurous    __ persuasive    __ ambitious    __ extroverted

__ aggressive    __ in control    __ demanding    __ argumentative

__ decisive    __ forceful    __ active    __ politically aware

<u>Part 3</u> Directions: From the list of Occupations and College Majors below, indicate those you think you would enjoy or find interesting with a √. *Do not worry if you lack the expertise or education to excel in these areas.*

__ Operations Manager__ County Auditor    __ Politician

__ Controller    __Tax Attorney    __ Purchasing agent

__ Communications    __ Real Estate    __ Business Management

__ Entrepreneurship    __ Retail Management __ International Marketing

<u>Directions for scoring:</u> Add all of the √s you made in each of the three parts. The total number of √s is your score on the Realistic Holland theme. Enter that total score below.

My raw score on the Enterprising theme is: _____ (Enter your total score)

This score falls within the _____ percentile range (Refer to chapter 7)

This score falls within the _____ category (Refer to chapter 7)

## Developmental advice

If your score on the "self-test" was in the *high* or *average* ranges, you may find some of the suggestions that follow helpful.

If you choose to work on any of these areas, do not attempt to do too much at once. Select *two* or *three* items. Enlist the support and encouragement of persons you respect in this process and seek their feedback and advice periodically.

1) Be alert to the possibility you may intimidate people who are under-confident, mild-mannered or shy. Do not come on too strong with such individuals.

2) Make sure you maintain a reasonable balance between pursuing career success and "success" in personal, non-work areas of your life.

3) Identify situations where your goals and those of the larger team or organization will be better served if you are less aggressive, more willing to compromise and less stubborn.

4) Establish challenging, yet reasonable goals for your team. Do not push anyone too hard for too long. Involve associates in goal setting and decision making to enhance their buy in.

5) Be diplomatic when expressing your strong opinions or withhold comment until you hear everyone's point of view. Foster open dialogue and do not end it prematurely.

6) Be open-minded and flexible when presented ideas that are different from your own. Look for the value in divergent points of view.

7) Ensure that you pay attention to small, but significant details as well as duties you find less interesting.

8) When making decisions, do not overlook short-term consequences. Consider how your decisions will affect various people who will be influenced by them. Explore their *feelings* about key decisions.

9)    As a manager, take time to offer praise and encouragement. Show patience when training or coaching others. Mentor someone who is quite different from you in personality and style.

10)   Carefully consider the potential negative consequences of employing competition among associates as a motivational tool. Explore other means to help your team and coworkers excel.

11)   Temper your competitiveness. Do not allow it to interfere with team work.

12)   Avoid acting or deciding in haste, simply to expedite a project or speed yourself along toward a goal.

**Final comment**

If your score on the self-test was in the *high* range, you may need to broaden your interests and become accepting of people who are different from yourself. People characterized by the Investigative theme would be most different from you in interests, personality and values. Re-read chapter 2 to learn about such people and their interests.

# CHAPTER 6

$\blacklozenge$

# CONVENTIONAL TYPES: "WE LIKE ORDER."

As indicated in the title of this chapter, Conventional types (*Cs*) of people like order. This is as opposed to their having mechanical interests, enjoying resolving complex problems, creating and using their imagination, or leading others. If given a choice, *Cs* would prefer to deal with other people who have a similar preference. This is not to say *Cs* are unable or unwilling to do other things, or interact with other types of people. They can, of course. However, they like to stick with their preferences if at all possible. Yet, *Cs* interests and preferences can take on a variety of forms. So too, can their abilities. Their personalities are also broader than might be inferred by the above comments. Let's take a look at what makes an *C* an *C*.

**Interpersonal style**

In relations with others, *Cs* are often introverted, quiet and mild-mannered. They are also generally pleasant, polite and considerate individuals. Yet, *Cs* do shy away from taking the social initiative on the job, and can have difficulty starting or holding up their end of conversations. This is particularly true when dealing with people they do not know well, or when operating in new environments.

Normally, *Cs* are agreeable and cooperative individuals who will readily help others needing assistance. Along with this, they are patient, and will take the necessary time to instruct or train coworkers if they have valuable knowledge, skills or experience to share. Because of their shyness, *Cs* can be difficult to get to know on a personal level, and to do so requires gentle persistence on the part of others. Yet, when they are comfortable in their surroundings, *Cs* are much more amiable. As friends, they are loyal.

Considering the foregoing discussion, *Cs* usually need to be encouraged or urged to speak during meetings and discussions. Otherwise, their ideas, interests and opinions can be overlooked. It is helpful to remind *Cs* they likely have information, a perspective, or a point of view others lack that is needed to "fill-out" a discussion. *Cs* must remind themselves of this fact, as well.

*Cs* prefer harmony and avoid discord or conflict with others, on or off the job. The flipside to this is, *Cs* can be too accommodating and accepting and are reluctant to stand up and fight for their ideas, needs or initiatives. If they suspect their concerns will meet with disapproval, rejection or objections, *Cs* are likely to remain silent and go along with others' wishes (outwardly, not necessarily *inwardly*). The same is true if they lack complete certainty their ideas are correct. However, internally, *Cs* are likely to be mildly critical of others, and upset with their own unwillingness to speak up and assert themselves.

As employees, *Cs* want to do the right thing. They respect authority, the established chain of command, and the decisions of superiors. *Cs* also take constructive feedback seriously, and will make a commitment to improving as indicated. Although they do not clamor for recognition and attention, *Cs* do appreciate other's gratitude for their effort, and a "thank you" means a lot to them.

## Talents, abilities and decision making

The abilities of *Cs* fall in the realm of working with numbers, details and assignments where accuracy is critical. They often have strong, basic mathematical and computational skills. Along with this, *Cs* typically have solid perceptual skills (the ability to work well with tasks requiring speed and precision). In addition, their manual dexterity skills may be quite strong compared to others. All of these attributes add up to an ability for *Cs* to excel in jobs requiring clerical or administrative work. They are similarly well-suited to work that demands precision and accuracy.

Furthermore, *Cs* are well focussed when working on problems, especially while gathering data and implementing solutions. Thus, they carefully attend to what they are doing and strive to be very methodical in the process.

As problem-solvers, *Cs* are deliberate, careful and strive to avoid making errors or mistakes. In addition, they will do a fine job handling routine, day-to-day decisions within their area of training or expertise. As employees, *Cs* are dependable individuals who make sure the often overlooked, or underrated, day-to-day work is properly completed. They are most often noticed in organizations *when they are not there*. Then, others may struggle to figure out the procedures, systems, et cetera, for getting typical daily tasks completed.

When it comes to problem solving, *Cs* do best handling day-to-day matters, as well as those that fall well within their training and realm of experience. They manage these efficiently, and are quick to note subtle differences that might suggest the need to gather additional information before finalizing their decisions. *Cs* are also effective resolving problems for which there are clear procedures to follow. In so doing, they closely adhere to established guidelines, and avoid setting unwanted precedents through their actions or decisions. When unsure of how to proceed, *Cs* will seek input from those they respect. *Cs* must guard against becoming bound by procedures, and recognize when to make appropriate exceptions to them. As it is, they tend to view rules as absolutes instead of guidelines. In a worst case scenario, this can lead to a stereotypical "bureaucratic mindset" wherein rules are rules and there are *no exceptions.*

In terms of their abilities, *Cs* are weaker when it comes to being creative, inventive or innovative. That is, they are most comfortable doing things in a standard or traditional way. As a result, they are slow to adapt to change and can have considerable difficulty seeing a problem or issue from a substantially different viewpoint. Similarly, they are rarely risk takers but instead, *Cs* can be much too cautious and careful making decisions. *Cs* are also less skilled when it comes to social interactions, especially those requiring persuasion or influencing others. Moreover, *Cs* are rarely strong, verbal communicators. They tend to be too brief when sharing information whether in writing or speaking.

## Work style and motivational factors

*Cs* are typically adept following procedures closely and proceeding through their work in an orderly fashion. Thus, when a project demands tasks be done according to a strict set of guidelines, *Cs* can be counted on to do exactly that. In fact, *Cs* welcome the challenge of such responsibilities. Likewise, they have a facility for handling routine work adeptly because they are disciplined, and consistent in their work habits.

In all of the above regards, *Cs* are well served by their strong attentional skills (that is, their ability to stay focused on what they are doing). They are impressive in their ability to work long periods of time on tedious tasks or assignments, demonstrating a good deal of focus and discipline in getting them done. *Cs* also take time to dot their "i's" and cross their "t's" in an effort to be as thorough as possible.

Another asset for *Cs* is their ability to be efficient moving through their work. Because they are conscientious and seek to develop good work habits, *Cs* are often able to improve or speedup the way they work by developing effective routines or methods where none may have previously existed. This reflects their orderly, methodical work style. As noted earlier, *Cs* are the often unnoticed individuals within organizations who keep things running smoothly by making sure necessary, but unglamorous work is done properly and on time.

*Cs* share an important interest with *Es*. Both are business minded. While *Es* mostly are concerned with broader scoped, big picture requirements and goals, *Cs* focuses on the smaller elements that are crucial in ensuring continuity within organizations. *Cs* demonstrate a concern for the bottom line, and do what they can to keep costs in line while using organizational resources carefully.

*Cs* function well as implementers. That is, they can be counted on to see plans through as outlined, and do what is expected of them in a dependable fashion. In subordinate roles, they are responsive, dutiful and compliant. If they need clarity regarding expectations, *Cs* will ask questions and show respect for the authority, decisions and experience of superiors. Thus, they are unlikely to challenge the thinking of their manager or those who are more experienced than themselves. Therein, however, is one of their shortcomings; a lack of assertiveness. Generally, *Cs* are hesitant to speak up during meetings or discussions. This is especially true when they lack one hundred percent certainty they are correct in their thinking or conclusions. Often, it will be up to others to draw the *Cs* views or ideas out with specific questions.

*Cs* value and are motivated by security, stability and predictability in relationships and work settings. They also value financial rewards, loyalty and fair-handed treatment by others. In addition, they operate best when goals, expectations and guidelines are *very* clear-cut and specific; conversely, *Cs* find ambiguity in their work and environment uncomfortable and frustrating. They will likely have difficulty doing their best if superiors are demanding (unfairly so), prone to put them under a lot of pressure or, for someone who is critical and not particularly supportive and patient. Finally, *Cs* do not prize or strive for positions of power, prestige or status.

## Leadership

In light of the prior discussion, it may be evident *Cs* are unlikely candidates for visible or pressured-filled leadership roles. Generally, they lack the boldness, aggressiveness and pure ambition and confidence required for such positions (in contrast to *Es*). They are skilled tacticians, not strategic thinkers, who focus on short rather than long-term goals.

This does not mean *Cs* cannot lead. Instead, it suggests the situation and setting in which they do lead, must be carefully chosen and "play to" their strengths. Thus, *Cs* can provide necessary direction to a team of other *Cs* or *Ss* and perhaps, *Is*. This is especially so if *Cs* are more capable, experienced or possess a higher degree of expertise compared to those they lead. *Cs* can perform well in these instances because other *Cs* as well as *Ss* and *Is* will not require a hard-charging, aggressive leader.

Typically, *Cs* lead via rules and procedures and rely upon the diligence and reliability of team members to get things accomplished. Likewise, *Cs* are helpful, considerate leaders who will readily assist associates who are struggling. They are also low-keyed and reserved in their style of leadership.

Employees who report to *C*-managers will discover they are appreciative of their work, but not particularly demonstrative conveying positive feedback. This suggests *Cs* must make a conscious effort to let others know they are pleased with their efforts and contributions.

As leaders, *Cs* can err by being too easygoing, and fail to be firm handling performance and personnel problems. These matters may be allowed to go on too long before they take action. When confronting such problems, *Cs* are apt to tone down their comments versus being direct, stating their concerns or observations. Associates who are independent minded or aggressive, may test the limits of a *Cs* patience. Yet, *Cs* can also exhibit a surprising lack of compassion when it comes to enforcing the steps in a company's disciplinary process. They are unlikely, in some cases, to take account of extenuating circumstances that might suggest they show greater flexibility, indicative of *Cs* strict adherence to rules.

One clear situation in which *Cs* can be effective leaders, is in bureaucratic or well- structured types of organizations. Examples of these would be local, state or federal government agencies. *Cs* strength and, indeed, confidence operating in these settings, flows from the predictability the rules, procedures and guidelines inherent in such organizations provide. *Cs* mastery of these rules gives them access to leadership roles in these organizations.

Yet, these settings can also create the necessary circumstances to reveal a potential flaw some *Cs* display, especially when they are in high-level positions. That is, a propensity to come across as stuffy, smug, or overly concerned with propriety (behavior *they* deem appropriate and acceptable). Moreover, *C*-leaders can overstress their belief in the importance of rules and doing things a certain way. Consequently, rules in effect, become their primary means for directing others and keeping them in line. Essentially, *Cs* risk substituting an emphasis on following rules for true leadership. Most people have come across individuals in organizations who insist things be done in a particular way, in a particular order, or in accord with a certain set of guidelines—even when those strictures cease to make sense or have outlived their usefulness. The voluminous paperwork demanded by some organizations to make decisions, is an example of a *Cs* influence gone awry. Essentially, it reflects an overly zealous bureaucratic outlook.

### Interests: occupational and academic

*Cs* prefer quiet activities that allow them to use their desire for neatness and order. Thus, many *Cs* are collectors who patiently catalog and organize their collections. They are not inclined towards participation in competitive pursuits and interests, nor strongly socially-oriented activities. *Cs* are likely to have a small circle of close friends with whom they interact and share interests. Other areas of interest or hobbies could include jigsaw puzzles, needlework and certain types of woodworking and crafts (detailed).

Oftentimes, *Cs* have an interest in what are considered the "finer things in life," such as wine tasting, dining at "fine" restaurants, et cetera.

## Occupational

*Cs* frequently pursue administrative or clerical roles within organizations and other positions that require careful attention to details. Bookkeeping, accounting, inspection, secretarial, programming, and assembly jobs would be good fits for them. *Cs* prefer occupations that keep them out of the limelight (or firing line) where there is structure, predictability and low-to-moderate levels of stress or pressure. Many *Cs* pursue jobs with governmental agencies and large corporations, but not high level management roles. *Cs* are not likely to pursue, or feel comfortable working in people-intensive occupations such as sales, high paced customer service roles or counseling.

## Academic

*Cs* like predictability, and perform best in well-structured programs of study. Because *Cs* are conscientious students, they can be effective in courses that require memorization of basic principles, operations or specific methods for problem solving. Oftentimes, *Cs* excel in basic mathematics and courses that are practical and fact based, not theory based.

Many *Cs*, like *Es*, are interested in business courses. Unlike *Es*, *Cs* are mainly interested in programs that prepare them for administrative, clerical, inspecting, accounting roles versus managerial roles per se. *Cs* will also enjoy certain course work that is technical in nature, for example, computer programming.

*Cs* are generally diligent students who pay close attention to all requirements for completing course work and academic programs. They are unlikely to be particularly social in a school setting, except, perhaps with respect to other students who are a part of their programs, or who share their outside interests.

## College programs that fall within the Conventional theme:

Accounting

Accounting and
Bookkeeping

Accounting and
Computing

Bookkeeping

Broadcasting Tech-
nology

Business Data En-
try Equipment
Operation

Business Data Periph-
eral Equipment Operation

Business Data
Processing

Business Data
Programming

Central Supply
Technology

Clerk-Typist

Correspondence Clerk

Court Reporting

Credit Collec-
tion Clerk

Data Processing

Dry Cleaning Services

Insurance Clerk

Legal Secretary

Library Assisting

Machine Bill-
ing, Bookkeep-
ing & Computing

Mail and Order Clerk

Medical Office Man-
agement

Medical Records
Technology

Medical Secretarial

Personnel Assisting

Printing Press
Operation

Receptionist and
Communica-
tions Systems

Secretarial and Related
Programs

Stenographic

Teller

Typing

Typing, Gener-
al Office & Re-
lated Programs

Waiter and Waitress
Services

**Self-test**

The following questionnaire is designed to help you determine how closely you match up with the Conventional Holland theme. You will be asked to check-off ("√") answers you think describe yourself or match your interests. *Do not be surprised if you √ many or only a few phrases or words on this questionnaire.* For each section, honestly respond to the questions. Do not hurry. Move at a comfortable, relaxed pace.

<u>Part 1</u>  Directions: Indicate with a √ which of the following phrases describe you on the job or come close to your views.

___   I look for ways to streamline workflow.

___   I prefer to follow a well-defined, structured plan.

___   I am comfortable accepting direction from others.

___   I am patient when completing routine, daily tasks.

___   I do not speak up enough in meetings or discussions.

___   Managers should see to it employees complete their tasks as outlined.

___   I have no difficulty complying with my supervisor's decisions even if I see things quite differently from them.

___   During discussions, I let others do the talking because I may not be altogether sure of myself.

<u>Part 2</u> Directions: From the list of words or phrases below, indicate with a √ those that are *descriptive of you.*

\_ efficient          \_ low-keyed       \_ thrifty         \_ procedural

\_ meticulous         \_ conforming      \_ follow rules     \_ quiet

\_ mild-mannered      \_ compliant       \_ risk averse      \_ attentive

<u>Part 3</u> Directions: From the list of Occupations and College Majors below, indicate those you think you would enjoy or find interesting with a √. *Do not worry if you lack the expertise or education to excel in these areas.*

\_ Building Inspector  \_ Cost Accountant     \_ Tax Preparer

\_ Bookkeeper              \_ Computer Operator  \_ Assembly-line Inspector

\_ Court Reporting        \_ Word Processing      \_Business Data Programming

\_ Personnel Assisting   \_ Legal Secretary        \_ Medical Office Management

<u>Directions for scoring:</u> Add all of the √s you made in each of the three parts. The total number of √s is your score on the Realistic Holland theme. Enter that total score below.

My raw score on the Conventional theme is: \_\_\_ (Enter your total score)

This score falls within the _____ percentile range (Refer to chapter 7)

This score falls within the _____ category (Refer to chapter 7)

## Developmental advice

If your score on the "self-test" was in the *high* or *average* ranges, you may find some of the suggestions that follow helpful.

If you choose to work on any of these areas, do not attempt to do too much at once. Select *two* or *three* items. Enlist the support and encouragement of persons you respect in this process and seek their feedback and advice periodically.

1)     Exhibit a greater willingness to assert your views and opinions. Do not hold back  simply because you suspect someone will object or you are not completely sure of yourself.

2)     Take an active role during meetings. Make a point of being the first person to speak more often.

3)     Periodically, review the underlying rationale for policies and procedures. Ask yourself if they are still valid. Bear in mind, rules are guidelines, not absolutes. Use them with greater flexibly.

4)     When resolving problems, consider potential solutions that are non-standard or innovative. Do not rule out trying some new ideas.

5)     Avoid allowing others to take advantage of your quiet, cooperative style. Say, "No" to requests for help when you are too busy. Negotiate for reasonable goals if supervisors demand too much.

6)     As a leader, do not assume too much responsibility personally. Delegate more and ensure you develop challenging goals for associates that cause them to *stretch*.

7)     If people let you down, hurt, or offend you, speak up and let them know this. Avoid keeping these feelings to yourself. Remember, others can only change if they receive such feedback.

8)     When making decisions and planning, develop a habit of projecting farther into the future. Consider the total picture, not just the details. Explore long-term ramifications beyond the current situation.

9)     Be careful not to fall into routines that no longer serve a useful or valid purpose.

10) Swiftly tackle performance and personnel problems on your team to prevent their spreading or worsening.

11) Do not go overboard in an effort to be thorough in your work. Be only as precise as you must be to avoid wasted effort.

12) Be proactive in developing your career. Make your aspirations known to people who can further them. Call attention to your contributions and accomplishments. Do not undersell *yourself.*

## Final comment

If your score on the self-test was in the *high* range, you may need to broaden your interests and become accepting of people who are different from yourself. People characterized by the Artistic theme would be most different from you in interests, personality and values. Re-read chapter 3 to learn about such people and their interests.

# CHAPTER 7

◆

# SUMMARIZING THE SELF-TESTS

Now that you have completed the six Self-Tests from chapters 1 through 6, it will be helpful to summarize all of your scores. Follow the instructions below to do exactly this.

Instructions: Simply enter your individual Holland theme scores below in the appropriate spaces under "My score."

| Holland theme | My score | Percentile range[a] | Category name[a] |
|---------------|----------|---------------------|------------------|
| R | _____ | _____ | _____ |
| I | _____ | _____ | _____ |
| A | _____ | _____ | _____ |
| S | _____ | _____ | _____ |
| E | _____ | _____ | _____ |
| C | _____ | _____ | _____ |

My highest score was for the _____-theme[b]
My second highest score was for the _____ -theme[b]
My third highest score was for the _____ -theme[b]

[a]Refer to Table 1, below
[b]If there are ties for any of these, insert the theme that occurs first in RIASEC

To use Table 1, you need to first calculate your total raw score on the self-tests from chapters 1 through 6. If you have not, return to these chapters and do so.

For each self-test, find the range your score falls within under the "My Score" heading. Next, move to the "Percentile Range" heading to the right that corresponds with your score. Finally, move to the "Category Name" heading to find the category name corresponding with your score. Enter this information in the appropriate place at the end of each self-test and in the chart above. Note: A higher score or percentile means a stronger similarity to that theme.

Table 1
Translating scores on self-tests into percentile ranges and category names

| My Score | Percentile Range | Category Name |
|----------|------------------|---------------|
| 0 - 4.5 | 1-14 | Very Low |
| 5 -10.5 | 15-34 | Low |
| 11-20.5 | 35-64 | Average |
| 21-26.5 | 65-84 | High |
| 27-32 | 85-99 | Very High |

# PART TWO

# TAKING A CLOSER LOOK AT YOURSELF

In an effort to develop a thorough understanding of your particular pattern of Holland scores, the chapters in Part Two explain what your top two scores mean when they are combined. It should be noted that few people are "pure" Holland types or best described by a single theme. Instead, most people are well described by two or three themes, corresponding with their highest two or three scores on a Holland-based test (such as the self-tests in this book).

In these chapters, fifteen possible pairings of the Holland themes are described. The unique strengths and potential shortcomings of each pairing are outlined. In addition, other sections discuss incompatible pairings, potentially extreme behavior and illustrative occupations and interests.

After reading through the chapter discussing your top two Holland scores, you are encouraged to turn to the chapter discussing your incompatible pairing. This can help you gain valuable insight into people with whom you share little in common, may have had conflicts with, or have had difficulty understanding in the past.

The final chapter of this section will guide you through the process of developing your personal profile and creating a developmental action plan to implement changes you may want to make.

## CHAPTER 8

◆

# REALISTIC-INVESTIGATIVE TYPES: INDIVIDUALISTIC

**Potential strengths**

+ Task focused and have a preference for working with things and ideas versus people.

+ Enjoy working independently once goals have been made clear; yet, can work well within a small group setting.

+ Cautious, risk aversive; yet, will try new ideas if it is clear they will succeed. They will make conservative projections when it comes to important decisions, so as to minimize costs.

+ Technically oriented with a pragmatic, logical, common sense view of things; similar in approach to problem solving. Effective at resolving practical problems that require logic, critical thinking and a down-to-earth outlook.

+     Interact comfortably with people who have similar interests, beliefs and values.

+     Maintain control over emotions when making decisions. They are objective.

+     Not easily convinced by emotional appeals, smooth talkers or manipulative individuals.

+     Interpersonally, they are unpretentious and forthright, not prone to exaggeration nor boastful behavior. Instead, they tend to be humble and unpretentious.

+     Typically, they are careful when completing detail-oriented assignments.

+     They possess strong work values.

## Potential shortcomings

-     Weak, social interaction skills; reserved, quiet, introverted; not particularly talkative, communicative. Slow to open up and express themselves. They can also tend to be too serious, basically all work, and no fun.

-     They are not likely to be polished communicators and may be overly brief and fail to elaborate enough or use technical jargon too frequently.

-     Can be impatient with people who do not quickly grasp ideas they readily understand.

-     Can seem unfriendly, unsympathetic and have relatively few friends or acquaintances on or off the job; slow to extend themselves to others.

-     Rarely allow their feelings or emotions to come out; others may not know what is on their mind when they are upset.

-     Make decisions without fully considering the effect on, or feelings of, others. As such, they can make decisions that are logically correct, but unsound from an interpersonal perspective.

-       Hesitant to take risks, slow to accept change. They must be con-
        vinced there are sound reasons for trying new ideas or different
        methods.
-       Likely to convey feelings of frustration or anger via sarcasm or
        other indirect means.
-       Once their mind is made up, they can be stubborn or difficult to
        dissuade.

## Other attributes

*       Do not aspire to positions of power, prestige. Yet, as a leader, apt
        to be dependable, consistent, respectful of other's experience and
        expertise.
*       They have a preference for some structure in their work and in
        relationships.
*       Able to persuade others by developing sensible arguments, based
        in facts, data and appealing to common sense considerations. Not
        easily persuaded by others, particularly through emotional or non-
        factual arguments; can be stubborn.

## Incompatible pairing

The opposite of the Realistic / Investigative is the Social / Enterprising
(or reverse) pair.

RIs find the ESs outgoing, extraverted style, frustrating and burden-
some, because they are reserved and serious minded or task focused. RIs
can become upset with the willingness to take risks exhibited by ESs or
their lack of caution. In comparison, RIs prefer to play it much safer or, at
least have a high degree of certainty, that a new idea or venture will succeed.
As well, RIs prefer clarity before moving forward with a decision, while
seeking to understand all factors or possibilities involved. They would prefer to take extra time for precision than make an avoidable mistake. ESs are

willing to trust their feelings, instincts and the available information when making decisions, which can seem hasty or irresponsible to RIs.

## Illustrative occupations

RI      Mechanical engineer
IR      Chemical engineer

## Illustrative interests

RI      Carpentry, model building, rock climbing
IR      Stargazing, recreational flying, weather observing

## Potentially extreme behavior

The following is a brief discussion of behavior this pair could exhibit under highly stressful or difficult situations, or as a result of allowing certain attributes to develop to an extreme. It should be noted that these behaviors are rarely apt to be exhibited and most people described by this pair of Holland themes will never exhibit them. This discussion is included to convey a deeper sense of the range of qualities each pair could display. By talking about extremes, it is possible to further illuminate typical behaviors, attributes, et cetera.

The RI can easily lose sight of other's feelings and emotional needs. Consequently, they can be or seem inconsiderate and uncaring. RIs can also be too quick to judge others negatively and can be quite stubborn. Furthermore, they may justify decisions or actions (logically and on the basis of practical considerations), that hurt others, instead of moderating such decisions by taking account of soft data (i.e., other's feelings). RIs can demonstrate a notable lack of empathy at times.

# CHAPTER 9

◆

# REALISTIC-ARTISTIC TYPES: RESOURCEFUL

## Potential strengths

+ Sensible regarding the need for change and trying new ideas, but must be persuaded to accept them through clear reasoning. Thus, they respect tradition, uphold rules and are willing to make necessary changes to them.

+ They are able to come up with practical, useful ideas that are not so much creative or innovative as they are well suited to the particular needs of a problem or situation. That is, they can be inventive.

+ Once a decision has been reached, they are determined to see it through. As a result, they can be resourceful overcoming difficulties or obstacles.

+ They have a down-to-earth quality that makes them approachable; yet, they are slow to fully open up, extend themselves, or take others into their confidence. In this regard, they are not easily taken advantage of by others.

+     While they are not aggressive, they will stand up for their beliefs when they have strong feelings about an issue; when doing so, they are forthright.

+     They do not stray too far from the work at hand, even though they can, occasionally, devote too much time and attention to interesting tasks and assignments.

+     They can be "artisan-like" in their work approach; take pride in what they do.

+     They are loyal to people whom they respect.

## Potential shortcomings

-     Dogmatic about certain of their deeply held ideals and beliefs. They can be stubborn once they have reached a conclusion; subjective feelings can negatively influence their ability to be objective at times.

-     While reasonably open to the need for change, they can be difficult to convince at times.

-     They may not display particularly effective oral, or written communication skills. They may rely too much on a "good" idea selling itself, versus working hard to persuade others.

-     Their conservative, cautious side can conflict with their openness to new ideas; similarly, their pragmatic outlook can conflict with their idealistic leanings. The combination of these can lead to inner tension that could take the form of non-specific anxiety.

-     Apt to focus too much on immediate concerns, issues or consequences of decisions, instead of being broad scoped and strategic in their outlook.

-     They are unwilling to take significant risks, despite having a creative side and good ideas. They want assurances new ideas will succeed.

- They prefer to operate independently and can become upset with scrutiny of their work or decisions.
- Occasionally, they are too spontaneous and direct expressing their displeasure or disagreement, especially when their emotions are running high.

## Other attributes

* They believe in the need for creativity to serve a purpose, and would disagree with pushing for art or new ideas for their own sake.
* They can serve effectively in a leadership position when directing the efforts of specialized, well trained artisans; they provide clear goals, offer necessary support and guidance, and give members of their team sufficient latitude.
* Not likely to feel comfortable working for a controlling boss who has a hands-on style. This sort of relationship can become frustrating for them.

## Incompatible pairing

The opposite of the Realistic / Artistic is the Social / Conventional (or reverse) pair. RAs find the SCs outgoing, extraverted style (relative to themselves) frustrating and tiresome. The unassertiveness and lack of directness of SCs can irritate RAs who are willing to say what is on their mind by comparison, especially given the propensity of As to be rather spontaneous. In addition, RAs are somewhat more open to trying new ideas compared to the cautious SCs. SCs also have a stronger need to socialize, talk and interact with people than do RAs.

## Illustrative occupations

RA    Concrete sculptor
AR    Merchandise displayer

**Illustrative interests**

RA      Wood carving, bonsai growing
AR      Preservation of historic buildings, juggling

**Potentially extreme behavior**

The following is a brief discussion of behavior this pair could exhibit under highly stressful or difficult situations, or as a result of allowing certain attributes to develop to an extreme. It should be noted that these behaviors are rarely apt to be exhibited, and most people described by this pair of Holland themes will never exhibit them. This discussion is included to convey a deeper sense of the range of qualities each pair could display. By talking about extremes, it is possible to further illuminate typical behaviors, attributes, et cetera.

RAs can experience considerable internal conflict as a consequence of opposing attributes residing within them. This includes reasonableness / stubbornness, conservatism / open-mindedness, idealism / realism, et cetera. For a thorough explanation of these and other differences between Rs and As, review chapters 1 and 3. If RAs fail to recognize and reconcile these polarities, they are likely to experience plenty of frustration. This could spill over into close personal relationships they develop, and create heightened tension within them. The resulting self-alienation they may feel could also lead to alienation from others. RAs could also experience considerable difficulty settling on a career choice in light of their diverse interests. For some RAs, this may result in frequent job changes.

# CHAPTER 10

◆

# REALISTIC-SOCIAL TYPES: LOYAL

## Potential strengths

+ They view relationships in pragmatic terms and prefer clarity regarding roles for themselves and others. Thus, they operate effectively in a structured, predictable environment.

+ They value integrity, fairness, respect and helpfulness in others. They are dependable individuals who follow through on promises and commitments.

+ Enjoy providing practical help, advice or service to people; want to do what is right by others; they are typically straightforward and well meaning.

+ Do a fine job when given concrete assignments where there is a tangible, measurable result of their efforts. They work cooperatively with others to achieve objectives.

+      Respect the chain of command as well as the authority, experience and decisions of superiors; dutiful, loyal and responsive subordinates.

+      Fulfill their obligations in a steady, consistent fashion. When necessary, will assume a leadership role if asked or needed, and will serve diligently.

+      They are sensible, caring leaders who assure that rules are followed and goals, expectations and roles are clear.

+      Cautious individuals, they avoid making precipitous or costly mistakes; operate within established guidelines and procedures.

+      They handle disagreements or conflict with concern for others' feelings. They will make tough decisions involving people after careful consideration. They will also feel bad for those who may be hurt by such decisions.

+      Likely to develop a small, but tight-knit group of friends, on and off the job.

+      In a leadership role, can be both results- and people-oriented. That is, if well balanced, they can be strong directing a small team by focusing on what must be accomplished, and the needs and feelings of those who must perform the work.

## Potential shortcomings

-      They can experience internal conflict when faced with making unpopular, but necessary decisions. They may agonize over such decisions, especially if someone may be hurt or offended.

-      Occasionally, they can surprise others with the strength of their opinions, or when expressing their displeasure to others. This is apt to happen when they allow frustration with others to build up, and a precipitating event occurs that "sets them off."

-      They can experience conflict between their feelings of friendship and concern for others, and the need to confront them over work or other matters.

- There is the potential for them to oversimplify people or relationship problems by missing subtleties or less obvious issues.
- When they are upset or frustrated, they may pull back from interaction with others, wanting to be alone until they sort through their feelings.
- It can be difficult for them to ask for help, and they may struggle too long on their own with a problem; yet, they can be too quick to help others and may put themselves behind in their own work as a result.
- They can narrowly define roles, at work and otherwise, according to tradition and past practice, and are slow to change in this regard. Others may feel constricted or pigeonholed.
- Apt to experience change as frustrating. They can be quietly resistant to it.
- They may seem inconsiderate or offend without meaning to by becoming too task focused.
- Can become frustrated with those they feel are not as hard working as themselves; apt to limit contact with, and reliance on, such individuals.
- At times, they can be misunderstood because they do not express themselves or their ideas and opinions fully or altogether clearly.

## Other attributes

* They have a strong need for security and stability in relationships and their work; in return they are loyal and supportive, apt to be long-tenured employees especially if they feel valued and needed.
* At times, they prefer to be or work alone; yet, they also enjoy other's company. Thus, they do best in jobs and relationships that provide time for each of these needs.

\*        Perform optimally in predictable environments where rewards are
fair and they are treated with respect. They are most comfortable
with structure versus ambiguity in their work.

\*        They sometimes believe their motives and intentions are misunderstood by others.

## Sources of conflict or tension for RS or SR pairs

The Realistic-Social pair is one of three unique combinations (the others being Investigative-Enterprising and Artistic-Conventional) in the
Holland scheme. If you recall, earlier in the text, this pair sits opposite
each other on the Holland hexagon, which means they are theoretic, as
well as true opposites in the Holland typology.

In practical terms, this means individuals who are described by the RS,
IE or AC pairs are likely to feel occasional tension, confusion, frustration
or anxiety because of the values or needs clashes flowing from the differences in these themes. These feelings are likely to be felt more often if a
person's first two theme scores are noticeably higher compared to their
third theme score. The reason for this, is that in such cases, the individual
is best described by the first two themes with considerably less influence
coming from the other themes. Therefore, any moderating effect the third
theme (or other themes) might have, is significantly reduced.

This is not to suggest RS (or IE or AC) pairs are destined for lives of
anxiousness. In reality, the intrapersonal conflict these individuals may
experience can be used constructively and channeled, so their lives become
more satisfying. In fact, the resolution of these conflicts can result in RS
types being open-minded, flexible and balanced in many respects. The key
is for these individuals to recognize and understand the nature of these
differences, and use them to their full benefit.

There are several bases for potential conflict within the Realistic /
Social pairs. The first and most obvious has to do with the basic orientations of these two themes. Rs prefer to work with things over people; Ss

are exactly the opposite. Thus, the R-component in this pair compels RSs to be less inclined to interact with people, which contrasts with the Ss attraction to people. There is a natural friendliness found in Ss while Rs can come across as insensitive to others at times. Similarly, Ss are nurturing and readily see the positive in others. Rs can come across as too quick to criticize, or note flaws in others. In the extreme, Ss can be naïve, overly trusting and easily taken advantage of by others. Rs can be overly suspicious, guarded and intolerant of those who have different values from their own.

Secondly, Rs are task focused and waste no time getting down to the work at hand. They often display a sense of urgency and impatience with those who seem to slow them down or do not demonstrate their obvious sense of duty. Ss want to make sure their environment is pleasant, and there is harmony among coworkers before beginning their work. They try to ensure everyone is comfortable, and will take time to chat or socialize before beginning an assignment. They often lack an obvious sense of urgency. Consequently, RSs can feel pulled between simply jumping into their work and taking some time to talk with coworkers. They can also feel conflicted by a desire to keep to themselves and get to know their fellow employees on a personal level. Once again, looking at extremes, the Rs can become focused on what must be done, and the Ss can become too involved in the social aspects of their jobs.

Thirdly, Rs are conservative in their orientation, views and opinions. As a result, they can be black and white or narrow in their thinking. Conversely, Ss are open-minded and much more flexible in their outlook. They can readily see different sides to an issue and are tolerant of differences in opinions, reflecting a liberal perspective. Not surprisingly, RSs can sometimes feel torn between being tolerant of divergent opinions and viewing issues from a limited perspective, while being unyielding and uncompromising.

Fourthly, Rs tend to be brief communicating their thoughts—men or women of few words. Ss enjoy talking and discussing ideas in depth. In fact, they make an effort to involve others in discussions even if it means extending a meeting longer. If Rs were present in such a meeting, they would become irritated and wish everyone would just get to the point. It is not unusual for Ss to frustrate others by being verbose and slow to make a point, while Rs can cause frustration because they do not offer enough information, do not communicate clearly, and can be much too direct.

Fifthly, Rs approach to decision making is direct and straightforward. They rely on the available information, their experience and common sense. They do not waste time deliberating or seeking others' opinions or ideas. Ss are consensual decision makers who do not want to take a chance of overlooking someone's views or suggestions, and prefer a high degree of certainty before finalizing decisions compared to Rs. Rs sometimes feel Ss lack common sense and a practical orientation; Ss view Rs as overlooking valuable input from others, and cutting off fruitful discussions by being hasty.

Finally, in relationships, Rs can be dominating or controlling and expect plenty of autonomy. They can also be resistive to direction from others. Ss are submissive and have a strong need to feel valued and appreciated. They tend to be too responsive to others and overly eager to please—to the point where they put others needs before their own. Resulting from these differences, RSs can feel frustrated if their actions or "freedom" on the job are limited, but also become upset if they do not receive enough recognition or praise.

The above differences between Rs and Ss are not a complete list, but do point out some major potential sources of intrapersonal conflict for people represented by RS pairs. These are differences or issues that such individuals need to be aware of and address in a constructive fashion as any of these issues, in and of themselves, can cause considerable anxiety and even lead to interpersonal or work and career dissatisfaction.

It should also be noted that the spread of scores among a person's first three themes from the highest to the lowest will speak directly to the potential for conflict as noted earlier. For example, if the R and S scores are close and the third theme is significantly different (lower), the above conflicts (one or more) are apt to be present and felt more intensely by such individuals. Conversely, if a person's first three theme scores are close to each other, the conflict is less likely and, where present, felt less strongly. This is a result of the moderating or attenuating influence the third theme can impart.

## Illustrative occupations

RS      Ambulance driver
SR      Occupational therapist

## Illustrative interests

RS      Camping, crossbow shooting
SR      Watching sporting events, jogging

## Potentially extreme behavior

The following is a brief discussion of behavior this pair could exhibit under highly stressful or difficult situations, or as a result of allowing certain attributes to develop to an extreme. It should be noted that these behaviors are rarely apt to be exhibited and most people described by this pair of Holland themes will never exhibit them. This discussion is included to convey a deeper sense of the range of qualities each pair could display. By talking about extremes, it is possible to further illuminate typical behaviors, attributes, et cetera.

The RS may stay in a "bad" relationship too long if a practical need (i.e., it offers some security) is served by doing so, instead of making a clean break and starting over. Likewise, they can stay in a poor work situation if it provides a high level of security and stability. The RS can experience considerable inner conflict and anxiety if they do not come to understand the opposing forces involved in being both an R and an S, and fail to take measures to ensure they satisfy the needs of each. If the R-side predominates, they may fail to be sufficiently reflective to take note of this conflict.

# CHAPTER 11

◆

# REALISTIC-ENTERPRISING TYPES: AGGRESSIVE

## Potential strengths

+ Convey confidence in themselves as well as their ideas and ability to deliver results; have the potential to be inspiring leaders who spur their team on to great accomplishments.

+ Take sensible risks and do all within their power to ensure their ideas and ventures succeed.

+ Possess an ability to come through under dire, difficult circumstances; some thrive on, or feed off, of pressure. Oftentimes, highly energetic people.

+ A natural ability to take charge and provide direction to others; establish challenging standards, goals and hold people accountable.

+ Extremely competitive, unwilling to accept second best; determined, display a will to overcome obstacles; unrelenting tenacity and perseverance.
+ Outgoing, take the initiative dealing with people, and put their best foot forward; may display "street smarts."
+ Aggressive, no nonsense interpersonal style; independent minded, firm and assertive. Have the will to make tough, even unpopular decisions when convinced such actions are justified and necessary.
+ Exceptionally driven and ambitious; do what it takes to get ahead and build a solid career. Capable of delivering impressive results; have the potential to attain a high-level management / executive position in production, manufacturing or sales organizations.
+ Influential, persuasive; have the ability to generate support and acquire resources needed to achieve difficult objectives. Do not easily accept "No" for an answer; develop logical arguments to support their ideas.
+ Capable of thinking strategically while developing a clear vision of what they want to accomplish. They also develop a realistic sense of what it will take to reach objectives. At their best, they can be both tactical and strategic in their thinking.
+ Can serve as a catalyst or driving force for change.

## Potential shortcomings

- May assume or "take" more authority than is inherent in their position. Can have difficulty serving in a subordinate role if they do not respect superior's capabilities or leadership style.
- Can be intimidating or overpowering, especially to unassertive, mild-mannered, under-confident people.
- Lack warmth, sympathy, tolerance for people; easily frustrated with those who do not deliver expected results. Difficult to regain their trust, respect or good graces if others let them down.

- When upset, can be blunt expressing their frustration.
- Come on much too strong for their ideas, needs and interests while relying on a hard sell approach. They can also be unyielding, and do not readily accept dissent or opposing views
- Can form opinions of others too quickly and on the basis of limited interaction and observation. Likewise, can come to conclusions or decisions in other matters just as quickly. They can be black and white thinkers.
- Because of their tremendous determination and confidence, they may be slow to cut their losses and stay with an unproductive idea or approach too long.
- Little tolerance for emotionally sensitive people; tend to view such qualities as signs of weakness.
- Easily frustrated by indecision or *seeming* indecision on the part of others.
- Can be or seem egocentric, cocky, arrogant; exhibit weak self-insight, but likely to over-accentuate their positive attributes.
- Quick to criticize others, slow to praise and offer encouragement; yet, they take critical comments personally. Can become defensive, or go on the offensive, when such feedback is offered.
- Neglect routine responsibilities in favor of those they find challenging, stimulating.

## Other attributes

* Prefer to work with highly self-motivated, confident people who display the same ambition and determination as themselves. They seek an environment that is results-oriented and where they have plenty of autonomy.
* They want to work on important projects and make an impressive contribution to the success of their organization. They must know there are many opportunities to advance within the company.

*     Too many such individuals on a team can be disruptive because they can become overly competitive with each other. Ill-suited to work in a service organization because of their aggressive, competitive nature.

## Incompatible pairing

The opposite combination of the Realistic / Enterprising is the Social / Investigative (or reverse) pair.

The raw aggressiveness of REs certainly clash with the reluctant, hesitant SI style. REs can intimidate SIs and become irritated with the propensity of SIs to carefully measure their opinions and decisions. REs are also extremely competitive, an attribute sorely lacking in any discernible measure within SIs. Consequently, REs often establish extremely challenging goals versus the comparatively modest expectations of SIs. Furthermore, REs are venturesome, bold and risk takers. They cannot fathom the lack of these attributes in SIs and will pressure such individuals to take chances, which leads to frustration and disappointment all around.

## Illustrative occupations

RE     General supervisor
ER     Director of research and development

## Illustrative interests

RE / ER     Auto rallying, drag racing

## Potentially extreme behaviors

The following is a brief discussion of behavior this pair could exhibit under highly stressful or difficult situations or as a result of allowing certain attributes to develop to an extreme. It should be noted that these behaviors are rarely apt to be exhibited and most people described by this pair of Holland themes will never exhibit them. This discussion is included to convey a deeper sense of the range of qualities each pair could display. By talking about extremes, it is possible to further illuminate typical behaviors, attributes, et cetera.

The ER can be so ambitious and driven that their family life and friendships can be neglected. They can also drive themselves and others too hard, which could lead to burn-out. Their lack of concern for others' feelings and needs can lead to alienation from those around them. In a work setting, this could produce high turnover for the staff of an RE manager. In personal relationships, it can result in divorce or estrangement from friends and family. When the need for power, control and authority become primary motivators for ERs, they can adopt a "win at any cost" mentality. Should this occur, ERs will take scant account of whether or not their actions are right or wrong if the desired goal is reached. In such situations ERs will surely believe that the means they employed justify the ends they achieved. In some instances, this can yield decisions of questionable ethical quality. Furthermore, the aggressive, risk-taking tendencies of ERs can produce significant financial losses when they latch onto an idea quickly, commit substantial monetary resources, and are reluctant to cut their losses as the venture begins to go "south."

# CHAPTER 12

◆

# REALISTIC-CONVENTIONAL TYPES: TACTICAL

## Potential strengths

+ Extremely pragmatic, the most pragmatic of all pairs; act on the basis of what makes sound common sense.

+ Bring structure, predictability to their work and environment; develop sensible routines to fulfill their responsibilities.

+ Disciplined in many respects; "artisan-like" in their approach to achieving results. Not easily distracted; demonstrate a lot of pride in what they do. Do a job right the first time.

+ Dutiful, reliable and dependable people. Consistently follow through on commitments. They can be taken at their word.

+ Can serve as the foundation for building a solid team, because they are dutiful and live up to commitments; do what is expected, and carry at least their fair share of the workload.

+ Cautious and avoid acting in haste. Most likely to take the safer of various routes; thus, they avoid costly errors.

+ Cost conscious, they look for value. Often careful in the use of resources; they prize quality, accuracy and thoroughness in whatever they do.

+ Principled, guided by firm, internal values and beliefs; they respect authority, rules, tradition and the chain of command.

+ Able to handle routine, tedious, slow-moving assignments well; meticulous and work within established rules and systems.

+ Aware of subtle, practical issues or details others could miss; not easily distracted from the work at hand.

## Potential shortcomings

- Task, work and "thing" oriented versus people focused; introverted, serious, uncommunicative. Tend to keep to themselves and are rather guarded—even distrustful of others.

- Strongly risk aversive. Resist change, new or innovative ideas, feeling threatened by these. Eschew liberal thinking; can be too tradition bound.

- Low tolerance for ambiguity, find uncertainty disconcerting and frustrating; often view problems and situations in narrow terms, (e.g., black/white, correct/incorrect, right/wrong).

- Can be compulsive in attention to details; unnecessarily perfectionistic; difficult to please because they establish very exacting standards.

- Downplay feelings and emotions to the point where they are denied, but they can build up and come out unexpectedly. Do not take account of others reactions or feelings when making decisions.

- Difficult to get to know because they do not readily open up and are slow to extend their trust or respect. Tough to regain their good graces when others let them down.

-     As supervisors, slow to praise; do not offer enough encouragement and lack insight into how to motivate employees.
-     Inflexible and reluctant to change plans or decisions once they have been made.
-     Weak communication skills. Assume too much of others while being overly brief getting their ideas across in writing and when speaking.

## Other attributes

*     Work best in environments where there is clarity regarding roles, goals, expectations, guidelines; prefer predictability, stability. They have a very strong need for security.
*     Preference for tangible, concrete tasks or assignments where results are measurable and timelines specific.
*     Prefer quiet surroundings because it helps them to concentrate on the work at hand.
*     Effective short-range planners with a tactical outlook.
*     Hands-on, roll-up-sleeves style of leadership; provide a solid example for others as well as clear guidelines. Fair when delivering performance feedback.

## Incompatible pairing

The opposite combination of the Realistic / Conventional is the Artistic / Social (or reverse) pair.

There is an obvious clash between the free-spirited, open-minded outlook of the AS and the conservative, inflexible views of the RC. ASs can view RCs as stubborn and closed-minded, while RCs feel ASs are wishy-washy, too willing to change their minds. Moreover, the creative approach to doing things indicative of the AS style, can strike the RC as a lack of practicality. Along with this, the emotionally sensitive AS can frustrate the RC with their need for encouragement, recognition and nurturing. When the RC takes a pragmatic view of a problem, the AS can feel the chance to experiment with new ideas is missed. The openness with which the AS discusses their feelings can take the RC aback and make them uncomfortable. When an AS wants to talk or socialize, the RC may see this as wasting time.

## Illustrative occupations

RC    Furniture assembly inspector
CR    Bookkeeper

## Illustrative interests

RC    Auto maintenance, herb gardening
CR    Collecting fishing lures, completing jigsaw puzzles

## Potentially extreme behavior

The following is a brief discussion of behavior this pair could exhibit under highly stressful or difficult situations, or as a result of allowing certain attributes to develop to an extreme. It should be noted that these behaviors are rarely apt to be exhibited, and most people described by this pair of Holland themes will never exhibit them. This discussion is included to convey a deeper sense of the range of qualities each pair could display. By talking about extremes, it is possible to further illuminate typical behaviors, attributes, et cetera.

RCs can be a loners who do not make enough of an effort to make friends or expand their circle of acquaintances. They can also deny their feelings too much to the point where they "lose touch" with themselves and their emotions. Moreover, RCs can fall in with extremist groups that lie far outside the mainstream, if their already conservative outlook takes on a radical tone. Their strict adherence to tradition can result in falling behind the times, while losing out on the benefits of important innovations or valuable new ideas. RCs sometimes develop such a narrow range of interests that they fail to grow sufficiently with respect to their knowledge, skills and abilities.

# CHAPTER 13

◆

# INVESTIGATIVE-ARTISTIC TYPES: IMAGINATIVE

## Potential strengths

+ Imaginative, idea-oriented people; can be very creative and this attribute emerges in many different ways. They are the most imaginative or creative of all pairs.

+ Reserved, but quietly engaging. Others are apt to find them interesting people who often have a fresh, unique perspective to share.

+ Able to draw out others' creativity because of their open-mindedness.

+ Flexible in their approach to getting things done; tend to be resourceful and willing to experiment with new, fresh, innovative ideas without taking unreasonable risks

+ Will work long and hard on projects they find challenging, interesting, stimulating; typically able to get new projects off to an enthusiastic start.

+ Tolerant of ambiguity; able to operate effectively if given vague or general direction.

+ Can be both logical and intuitive in their approach to resolving problems.

+ Provided their communication skills are adequate, they can be persuasive, using reasoning and emotion to appeal to others, while presenting their ideas in an interesting and compelling fashion.

+ Strong in their ability to think conceptually; they are divergent thinkers.

+ Can be thorough handling work or assignments that capture and hold their attention.

+ Capable of viewing projects from a big picture perspective.

## Potential shortcomings

- Without specific deadlines or timelines, can become too caught up in interesting work to the detriment of other priorities; prone to overwork tasks they enjoy and find stimulating.

- May "reinvent the wheel" by pursuing creative ideas when existing approaches are likely to work effectively; can overlook practical considerations such as cost / time constraints, if their creative, intuitive side prevails.

- As problem solvers, can get lost in a sea of ideas, and have difficulty bringing things to closure. May put off decisions if they lack complete information or their curiosity is piqued by a new path of inquiry; sometimes undertake more research than necessary.

- Their preference for variety and stimulation can cause them to become bored with routine, necessary work; this could lead to procrastination in these areas.

- Can lose sight of overall goals or the larger picture by focusing too much on interesting or enjoyable activities or tasks.

- Frustrated with people who question their ideas or point out flaws in them; apt to interpret this as resistance to change or overly-conservative thinking.
- Can be expressive, but not assertive; neither are they aggressive, representing their ideas, needs or interests.
- Could have some weaknesses with regard to their social interaction skills; may be too reserved or seem aloof. They are sensitive to criticism.

## Other attributes

* They love sensory and mentally stimulating ideas, tasks, projects; prefer variety in their work.
* While not necessarily outgoing or particularly expressive verbally, neither are they asocial or overly restrained. They can be animated when speaking.
* Comfortable working in an interesting, visually, and otherwise, environment where free thinking and innovation is valued.
* They want room for autonomy; unlikely to perform well or feel comfortable in a structured, top-down or restrictive organization or environment.

## Incompatible pairing

The opposite of the Investigative / Artistic combination is the Enterprising / Conventional (or reverse) pair.

IAs find the ECs strong need for control, frustrating and self-limiting. This is especially apparent when the IA is well-trained or versed in a certain area, and the EC does not offer them sufficient autonomy. The same feeling of frustration can be experienced with respect to the ECs demanding standards, and resistance to ideas IAs find innovative. The need for order, rules and procedures of the ECs can also be a source of irritation for IAs. In this regard, IAs want some room for discretion when making decisions. Additionally, the directness of the EC, particularly when it comes to criticism, is upsetting to IAs. To the extent IAs view ECs as stubborn or exerting too much authority, they can become quietly resistive to their ideas or direction.

## Illustrative occupations

IA      Art appraiser
AI      Architect

## Illustrative interests

IA      Star photography
AI      Collecting art

## Potentially extreme behavior

The following is a brief discussion of behavior this pair could exhibit under highly stressful or difficult situations, or as a result of allowing certain attributes to develop to an extreme. It should be noted that these behaviors are rarely apt to be exhibited, and most people described by this pair of Holland themes will never exhibit them. This discussion is included to convey a deeper sense of the range of qualities each pair could display. By talking about extremes, it is possible to further illuminate typical behaviors, attributes, et cetera.

IAs can be terrible procrastinators with respect to their work and decision making. In this regard, they rely too much on their interests when establishing priorities, while over-looking practical considerations. Thus, IAs can downplay uninteresting, but necessary responsibilities. In addition, they tend to put off making decisions because they have difficulty narrowing down the list of options and keep the idea-generating process going too long. In addition, IAs can seem insensitive to others' needs on the job. This can happen when the way they use their time and set priorities conflicts with others' needs and requirements. That is, they can waste time by focusing too much on unimportant, but enjoyable or interesting activities, while being able to convince themselves the time was not wasted. In the process, others' needs can be inadvertently overlooked.

# CHAPTER 14

◆

# INVESTIGATIVE-SOCIAL TYPES: CAUTIOUS

**Potential strengths**

+ Potentially, both intuitive and logical in their approach to problem solving; willing to trust their inspirations. Open-minded, flexible and will consider others' ideas—even if different from their own.

+ Strong consultative and interpersonal skills; good feel for dealing with people. Diplomatic when handling conflict, disagreements; resolve these amicably, logically. Perceptive observers of people and attentive listeners.

+ Likely to have strong, verbal skills, both oral and written. Able to persuade others with tact, facts, solid reasoning and an appeal to others needs; anticipate objections in advance.

+ Can be strategic both when planning and in relations with others.

+     While they will disagree with others, they avoid heated discussions and do not burn bridges between themselves and others.

+     Patient with important details and slower moving projects. They develop thorough plans while looking ahead and anticipating potential problems.

+     Supportive and encouraging of others; facilitative when managing projects and people. They will offer praise, credit for a good job or effort.

+     Service-oriented helpers who enjoy providing assistance via counsel, advice and their technical ability and knowledge.

+     Normally able to grasp technical information and concepts readily.

+     Avoid making costly mistakes because they are cautious and do not take unwarranted chances.

## Potential shortcomings

-     Not assertive or aggressive enough dealing with people; apt to compromise too readily to avoid a confrontation. Hesitant to boldly say what they think. They can equivocate instead of being straightforward; reluctant to directly challenge other's ideas.

-     Overly responsive to others; too quick to lend a hand. Thus, they can fall behind in their own work; tend to be too accommodating versus pushing for their own needs, interests and agendas.

-     May overcomplicate problems, people and others, while taking in more information than they need to arrive at a reasonable conclusion; apt to undertake more research than is needed. This is especially true if they are operating under loose or no time constraints.

-     May fail to display a strong sense of urgency. Can push deadlines which will frustrate others; apt to overwork less critical, but interesting tasks and assignments.

-     There could be an element of aloofness to their interpersonal style when they are in new situations, meeting new people or in general.

- Slow to reprimand, criticize or discipline others when it is warranted; prone to soft-pedal negative feedback and water it down; their good nature and easygoing style can be taken advantage of by others.
- Too optimistic assessing others' abilities, and inadvertently expect too much; overly favorable when evaluating others' work, performance.
- May miss out on some opportunities by being too careful or deliberate in their actions and decisions.
- Somewhat idealistic and not always pragmatic. This can emerge as naïveté in interpersonal relationships.
- Sensitive to criticism, but unlikely to be open, expressing their feelings or disagreement; tend to carefully review such feedback to determine its veracity.

## Other attributes

* If serving in a management position, likely to create a participative, flexible, supportive environment where learning is emphasized; can be patient teachers or coaches.
* Work best in a collegial environment where everyone works cooperatively to achieve mutual goals; do not care for competitive settings or those that are hard-driving and bottom-line oriented.
* Motivated by a desire to learn, grow and achieve their full potential, personally and professionally.
* Though they are not especially ambitious, they are interested in advancing if it means learning and developing themselves and others.

## Incompatible pairing

The opposite of the Social / Investigative combination is the Realistic / Enterprising (or reverse) pair.

SIs exhibit concern for the needs of others, whereas REs exhibit a lack of sensitivity for people's feelings. In situations where both pairs exist on a team, SIs will become upset with this attribute in REs without confronting them, resulting in increasing tension between them. At some point, the situation could reach a boiling point, wherein the SI unexpectedly vents their frustration, but perhaps, in an inappropriate fashion. SIs find the unwillingness of REs to develop mastery over a body of knowledge before making important decisions troubling. Yet, SIs can also take too much time making up their minds, which frustrates REs. SI managers' fair minded and tolerant style can be taken advantage of by aggressive, forceful, sometimes, manipulative REs

## Illustrative occupations

SI      Counseling psychologist
IS      Pediatrician

## Illustrative interests

SI / IS  Peace organization membership, tutoring

## Potentially extreme behavior

The following is a brief discussion of behavior this pair could exhibit under highly stressful or difficult situations or as a result of allowing certain attributes to develop to an extreme. It should be noted that these behaviors are rarely apt to be exhibited and most people described by this pair of Holland themes will never exhibit them. This discussion is included to convey a deeper sense of the range of qualities each pair could display. By talking about extremes, it is possible to further illuminate typical behaviors, attributes, et cetera.

The SI can be too tolerant, easygoing and reserved for their own good. Thus, their good nature and trust can be abused. Others may also push or test the limits of their patience and empathy. SIs can make decision making extra difficult by involving too many people in the process, analyzing too much, or deliberating too long. The SIs reflective, introspective tendencies can be frustrating to those around them, especially people who are naturally decisive. As well, their propensity to downplay conflict, compromise and be diplomatic can backfire, and make a situation much worse, whereas a firm approach would have yielded much better results. Beyond this, they can put off finalizing difficult decisions that could upset other people.

# Chapter 15

---◆---

# Investigative-Enterprising Types: Strategic

**Potential strengths**

+ Quick-minded individuals; they are able to rapidly size up problems and can be decisive, able to readily see flaws in others ideas and thinking. The most logical of all pairs.

+ Appropriately assertive. Will take a stand on important matters; have the ability to overcome objections on the basis of sound, logical arguments.

+ Typically possess strong communication and language skills; express themselves effectively in writing and when speaking.

+ They are competitive; yet, sufficiently well restrained to keep this instinct in check. Thus, able to channel this energy into positive, productive pursuits.

+     Reasonably flexible in their approach to achieving results. That is, they operate logically, will make necessary adjustments to plans and decisions to achieve objectives.

+     Willing to take measured, well-calculated risks; experimental outlook; open to making bold changes / decisions provided there is data and sound logic for doing so.

+     Capable of seeing the bigger picture and how the details must fit to complete it; the most strategic of all pairs.

+     Can be persuasive by developing solid, compelling arguments; do a fine job of presenting their ideas; can be firm and forceful when they strongly believe in their ideas—even in the face of opposition.

+     Strategic in relations with others and in building a network of contacts they can draw upon when they need information and/or support.

+     Comfortable dealing with ambiguity; able to sort through it and make headway; can be impressive in their ability to work long hours in order to resolve a difficult problem.

## Potential shortcomings

-     Can be insensitive to other's feelings. This is especially true when they are working on a difficult problem or are focused on a challenging project.

-     Could become too immersed in intellectually stimulating projects or responsibilities; consequently, priorities, duties, responsibilities they deem unimportant or unchallenging can be overlooked.

-     Impatient with people who do not catch on quickly, especially in areas they readily understand. May intimidate those who do not have their technical skills and knowledge.

-     Apt to become frustrated quickly if they cannot readily resolve a problem on their own, or must rely on others too much for help.

- May make routine or day-to-day decisions too quickly without considering all available data or options. Focus too much on intriguing problems while devoting insufficient time to less interesting matters; Do not pay enough attention to the short-term or tactical components of decisions.
- Easily bored by unchallenging projects or priorities; likely to rush through these. Interest drops off when their projects fall into the latter or maintenance stages.
- Can overrate others' capabilities and demand too much of them. This is most likely if they are very intelligent or quite capable themselves. They can transfer their high self-expectations onto others.
- May experience inner conflict as a result of being results- and action-oriented, as well as concerned with producing top-quality work.
- Their need for restraint and emotional control can conflict with their expressive, assertive and competitive propensities, resulting in inner tension.
- Can be too competitive at a cognitive, intellectual level. For example, wanting their ideas to win-out over others, resulting in stubbornness.

**Other attributes**

* Particularly well-suited to project work where they must direct a technical or scientific team.
* Ambitious; comfortable assuming a leadership position; provide a clear vision and determine a logical route to bringing it to fruition. They will hold others to high standards.
* Prefer an intellectually stimulating environment where they can innovate and have plenty of autonomy. Prefer to work for someone they can learn from who provides ongoing challenges, and values their ideas, but does not supervise too closely.

## Sources of conflict or tension for IE or EI pairs

The Investigative-Enterprising pair is one of three unique combinations (the others being Realistic-Social and Artistic-Conventional) in the Holland scheme. If you recall earlier in the text, this pair sits opposite each other on the Holland hexagon, which means they are theoretic, as well as true opposites in the Holland typology.

In practical terms, this means individuals who are described by the IE, RS or AC pairs, are likely to feel occasional tension, confusion, frustration or anxiety because of the values or needs clashes flowing from the differences in these themes. These feelings are likely to be felt more often if a person's first two theme scores are noticeably higher compared to their third theme score. The reason for this, is that in such cases, the individual is best described by the first two themes with considerably less influence coming from the other themes. Therefore, any moderating effect the third theme (or other themes) might have is significantly reduced.

This is not to suggest IE (or RS or AC) pairs are destined for lives of anxiousness. In reality, the intrapersonal conflict these individuals may experience can be used constructively and channeled so their lives become satisfying. In fact, the resolution of these conflicts can result in IE type being open-minded, flexible and balanced in many respects. The key is for these individuals to recognize and understand the nature of these differences, and use them to their full benefit.

There are several bases for potential conflict within IE pairs. First of all, Is enjoy and prefer working alone and do not have strong social needs. Es often seek out and prefer jobs and careers that revolve around social interactions. They thrive on dealing with people, and receive considerable satisfaction from this component of their work. In fact, Is can become worn down by too much people contact, whereas Es are energized by it.

Secondly, Is are cautious and reserved in relations with others. They are also slow to warm up or extend themselves. Other people may describe Is as unsociable as well. Es, on the other hand, are socially venturesome, bold and aggressive. They are sometimes described by others as being overly confident or too self-promoting. Similarly, where Is are unlikely to express their ideas or opinions unless they can support them, Es are comfortable saying what they think, whether or not their ideas or views have a sound foundation in fact.

Thirdly, Is are conscientious, concerned with being accurate and pay careful attention to important details. But, they can become too engrossed in interesting, but less critical priorities, and lose sight of the overall scheme of things. Es are much the opposite. That is, they can overlook details because they focus too much on the bigger issues.

Fourthly, in their way of thinking, Is are methodical, deliberate and do not reach hasty conclusions. They are also risk aversive and distrust hunches or feelings as a basis for decisions. Consequently, Is can be overly analytical. Es are decisive individuals. They seek to find answers and solutions as quickly as possible, and can be impetuous or rash at times. Additionally, Es will trust their instincts if they lack complete information or data, and are venturesome in their outlook.

Fifthly, Is are motivated by a desire to excel in a chosen field of interest and master a set of skills. They are also motivated by a need to learn, along with curiosity, but do not aspire to leadership positions per se. Es are ambitious individuals who want to achieve prominent positions of authority; the particular field of endeavor is not as important as career growth. They are motivated by prestige, power and status. Es do not enjoy being in subordinate positions.

Finally, Is communication style reflects a desire to be precise. They will tend to provide more, rather than less information to ensure this. Is prefer to have facts in hand to support their decisions or opinions, and will do their homework carefully. Es are comfortable talking "off-the-cuff" without prior preparation. They say what they think without concern for the facts being "just right." In addition, Es may assume too much of others when speaking, and fail to provide enough detailed information.

The above differences between Is and Es are not a complete list, but do point out some major potential sources of intrapersonal conflict for people represented by the IE dyad. These are differences or issues that such individuals need to be aware of, and address in a constructive fashion, as any of these issues, in and of themselves, can cause considerable anxiety and even lead to interpersonal or work and career dissatisfaction.

It should also be noted that the spread of scores among a person's first three themes, from the highest to the lowest, will speak directly to the potential for conflict as noted earlier. For example, if the I and E scores are close, and the third theme is significantly different (lower), the above conflicts (one or more), are apt to be present and felt more intensely by such individuals. Conversely, if a person's first three theme scores are close to each other, the conflict is less likely and, where present, felt less strongly. This is a result of the moderating or attenuating influence the third theme can impart.

## Illustrative occupations

IE     Director of quality control
EI     Production engineer

## Illustrative interests

IE / EI   Backgammon, chess

## Potentially extreme behavior

The following is a brief discussion of behavior this pair *could* exhibit under highly stressful or difficult situations, or as a result of allowing certain attributes to develop to an extreme. It should be noted, that these behaviors are rarely apt to be exhibited and most people described by this pair of Holland themes will *never* exhibit them. This discussion is included to convey a deeper sense of the range of qualities each pair could display. By talking about extremes, it is possible to further illuminate typical behaviors, attributes, et cetera.

IEs can be arrogant. They can overrate their own ideas and capabilities. If this occurs, their E-side can further dominate, and cause them to take unwarranted risks on the basis of insufficient analysis, especially with respect to tactical considerations. IEs can become so caught up in their work that other areas of their lives can suffer commensurately, particularly personal relationships. At the same time, IEs can overlook people's feelings and emotions when making decisions. Consequently, they may make technically or logically correct, but otherwise, unwise decisions from a human perspective. This could lead to alienation of their team. IEs can experience considerable inner conflict and anxiety if they do not come to understand the opposing forces involved in being both an I and an E and fail to take measures to ensure they satisfy the needs of each.

# CHAPTER 16

◆

# INVESTIGATIVE-CONVENTIONAL TYPES: PERFECTIONISTS

**Potential strengths**

+ Very precise, thorough and detail-oriented; can be counted on to dot their "i's" and cross their "t's."

+ Complete their work in an orderly, systematic fashion; do a fine job with tedious tasks, assignments requiring focused attention and patience.

+ Make few costly errors because they do not rush things nor act in haste; strong concern for quality; carefully recheck their work to catch errors or mistakes.

+ Tend to remain well-focused on the immediate work or problem at hand; stay with an assignment until it is properly completed.

+     Logical, analytical thinkers. They keep feelings and emotions out of the decision- making process and focus on facts, data and other objective elements.

+     Reliable, dependable workers; display a high level of discipline on and off the job; consistently follow through on their work, promises and commitments.

+     Dutiful, responsive individuals, especially in a subordinate role.

+     Enjoy adding to their current knowledge and skills, and applying what they have learned.

+     Work well within guidelines or parameters established for their jobs.

+     May develop into resident experts in certain areas of their jobs; others will value them as resources to turn to when they need information.

## Potential shortcomings

-     Extremely perfectionistic. Can go overboard in their attention to details, which can significantly slow down decisions and projects.

-     Unassertive; unwilling to speak out and argue for their ideas or interests; acquiesce or compromise too readily reflecting a strong desire to avoid disagreements or conflicts.

-     Lack interpersonal versatility; hesitant in relations with others; can be painfully shy, quiet, reserved; too withdrawn versus open.

-     Rarely trust their instincts even when they are accurate or represent good ideas; apt to have self-doubts about their own abilities.

-     Can focus so much on details and the immediate task at hand that they lose the forest for the trees; not broad scoped or visionary in their thinking.

-     They keep critical comments to themselves when others' actions warrant such feedback, instead of openly expressing them; can be difficult to get to know on a personal basis.

- Too cautious in their actions and decisions; tend to bypass creative, innovative ideas if they contain an element of risk or uncertainty.
- Follow rules, formulas and procedures too closely and rarely will make an exception to them. This can be frustrating to others working with them.
- Do not call attention to their achievements. Consequently, they can be overlooked and others may receive credit for their work or ideas.

## Other attributes

* They are mainly interested in things or ideas and task-focused than people-oriented.
* Tend to respect accepted practices and procedures as a way to achieve results, and have the potential to refine existing systems or methods.
* Work best in an unhurried job and environment where they can take sufficient time to be precise and thorough.
* Not likely to perform well or feel at ease in a production environment, a bottom-line operation or one that is hard-charging and extremely competitive; would not do well in a role demanding quick decisions and creativity; apt to feel comfortable in a technical or scientific (e.g., laboratory) environment.
* Shy away from visible leadership positions; do not care for the limelight and added pressure such roles entail. They are not driven by a desire to advance, but enjoy learning and seek security and stability.
* From an interpersonal standpoint, they are understated.

## Incompatible pairing

The opposite of the Investigative / Conventional combination is the Enterprising / Artistic (or reverse) pair.

ICs are inclined to view EAs as careless innovators who are overly eager to champion a new idea. They tend to feel EAs are too quick to support new, untried methods rather than analyzing them thoroughly and in considerable detail. ICs are too demanding when it comes to completing tasks or making decisions in accord with established and well-tested procedures in comparison to EAs. In contrast, EAs are willing to bypass procedures if they deem it necessary or expedient to do so. EAs are expressive and open, sharing their ideas, feelings or opinions, whereas ICs hold their emotions in and are reluctant to state their opinions. ICs have a difficult time swaying EAs to their way of thinking, even when they are correct, because they do not convey their views or opinions with enough enthusiasm, emotion or excitement.

## Illustrative occupations

IC      Internal auditor
CI      Accounting clerk

## Illustrative interests

IC / CI  Collecting scientific equipment

## Potentially extreme behavior

The following is a brief discussion of behavior this pair *could* exhibit under highly stressful or difficult situations or as a result of allowing certain attributes to develop to an extreme. It should be noted that these behaviors are rarely apt to be exhibited and most people described by this pair of Holland themes will *never* exhibit them. This discussion is included to convey a deeper sense of the range of qualities each pair could display. By talking about extremes, it is possible to further illuminate typical behaviors, attributes, et cetera.

CIs can be extremely introverted and lacking in confidence, generally and, particularly in relations with others. This can hurt them insofar as career growth and satisfaction with their work are concerned. In fact, CIs consequent lack of progression within their chosen vocation or career field can further fuel a lack of confidence. These attributes also hurt CIs when it comes to making friends and contacts outside of work, possibly leading to feelings of loneliness or alienation. Furthermore, CIs perfectionism can lead to extreme reluctance to make decisions because of their desire to eliminate all possible risks, and make sure they are absolutely correct in their actions. Related to this, CIs can substitute rules, policies, procedures and established formulas for true critical thinking, and in-depth analysis when making decisions.

# CHAPTER 17

◆

# ARTISTIC-SOCIAL TYPES: EMOTIONAL

## Potential strengths

+    Warmly enthusiastic in relations with others; sensitive to coworker's feelings, very intuitive in this regard.

+    Creative, imaginative individuals; able to look at problems and issues from a new, fresh perspective.

+    Open to change, especially if it facilitates harmony, cooperation and teamwork.

+    Flexible in their outlook and in their way of doing things; open to ideas and suggestions from others.

+    Nurturing individuals; sympathetic to coworkers especially those who are having difficulties. They take a personal interest in the people around them; able to soothe the feelings of people who have been hurt or offended.

+    Expressive in many different ways: visually, verbally, creatively.

+    If placed in charge of a team, they are approachable, considerate, facilitative, try to use the unique talents of others. They encourage growth and creativity; patient teachers especially with willing students.

+    Oftentimes, fun-loving individuals who want to enjoy whatever they are doing and see to it others do as well.

+    Convey plenty of enthusiasm for responsibilities, assignments or projects that capture their imagination; they work hard to excel in these areas.

+    Often display a service-oriented outlook and enjoy assisting, helping and teaching others.

## Potential shortcomings

-    They allow subjective factors, such as their feelings and emotions to cloud their thinking; thus, they are not always or often objective. They are the most emotional of all pairs.

-    Can fail to be sufficiently logical or calculating when evaluating problems or making decisions.

-    Display naïveté, which flows from a romantic/idealistic outlook; thus, can be too trusting and fail to take a realistic view of relationships, personal and work-related. They can be taken advantage of by those who are shrewd, manipulative, and worldly.

-    When they have been hurt or offended, can be slow to rebound, and take criticism or seemingly negative comments too personally.

-    They place others needs first; can be too accommodating versus assertive; do not fight back nor press for their ideas or needs.

-    Tend to be moody or temperamental while wearing their feelings on their sleeves; it takes a while for them to sort through their feelings when upset or disappointed.

- As managers, can become too close to those they supervise; may allow the halo effect to taint their objectivity when evaluating others' performance.
- Prefer to avoid controversy; reluctant to boldly lay their views on the line for fear of criticism or being challenged; unassertive in an upward direction.
- May lack a deep well of emotional and/or physical energy and resilience to draw upon when the road ahead is long, tiring and frustrating.

## Other attributes

* In relationships and work settings, need to feel valued, appreciated to do their best; have a strong need for recognition, support and encouragement.
* Work well in a warm, inviting, non-critical environment that is comfortable and visually appealing.
* Do not aspire to positions of control, power, influence; yet, their strong need for recognition can cause them to strive for a leadership role. Their desire to do something worthwhile for others can also influence such a decision.
* Have a difficult time dealing with people who are aggressive, forceful, no-nonsense like; uncooperative or inattentive to their feelings.

## Incompatible pairing

The opposite combination of the Artistic / Social is the Conventional / Realistic (or reverse) pair.

The no-nonsense, straightforward style of CRs is difficult for ASs to handle. This is particularly true as it also relates to the tendency of CRs to be intolerant and unsympathetic. The CR finds ASs need for recognition, praise and encouragement difficult to meet. Moreover, the directness of

CRs when offering criticism, can wound the ASs pride and hurt their feelings—even more than may be apparent. The AS can sometimes feel taken for granted or advantage of by the task-focused CR. CRs may feel ASs are not disciplined enough fulfilling their responsibilities, or sufficiently well-organized and systematic. Moreover, ASs can view the tradition-bound, conservative CR as too stodgy, stubborn or resistant to new ideas.

## Illustrative occupations

AS     Drama coach
SA     Career counselor

## Illustrative interests

AS     Concert going, portrait painting
SA     Playing charades, pen pals

## Potentially extreme behavior

The following is a brief discussion of behavior this pair *could* exhibit under highly stressful or difficult situations or as a result of allowing certain attributes to develop to an extreme. It should be noted that these behaviors are rarely apt to be exhibited and most people described by this pair of Holland themes will *never* exhibit them. This discussion is included to convey a deeper sense of the range of qualities each pair could display. By talking about extremes, it is possible to further illuminate typical behaviors, attributes, et cetera.

The AS can make poor decisions in relationships, finances, and, otherwise, on the basis of feelings, without looking at things logically and objectively. Likewise, ASs can focus too much on the immediate consequences of their decisions and not enough on the long-term ramifications. They can also be manipulated by shrewd, street-smart types on the basis of their feelings and emotions. In addition, ASs can be very moody or temperamental, leading to inconsistencies in various areas of their lives. Moreover, they are overly idealistic, naïve and insufficiently realistic in their orientation to the world around them. This can "set them up" for some tremendous disappointments in life and relationships.

# CHAPTER 18

————————— ◆ —————————

# ARTISTIC-ENTERPRISING TYPES:
# EXPRESSIVE

## Potential strengths

+ They can be creative in bold, striking ways; free-thinking, experimental and willing to try new things; can serve as a catalyst for change and inspire others to be creative.

+ Risk takers who can have both impressive successes *and* failures; undaunted from taking chances in the future if they have not succeeded previously.

+ Become excited over new, innovative ideas, can easily get others as excited; persuasive, can sell ideas in a compelling fashion employing catchy enthusiasm.

+ Do not easily accept "no" for an answer; readily promote themselves, their ideas and make the process of winning others over fun.

+     Able to see broad, sweeping vistas and are forward-looking and visionary.

+     Extraverted, outgoing, expressive (verbally and otherwise); the most expressive of all pairs.

+     Create enthusiasm at the start up of new projects, and are capable of getting them off to a fast start.

+     They encourage and can inspire others to be imaginative and innovative in their thinking.

+     Capable of bringing dramatic change to departments or organizations, especially those that have fallen behind the times.

+     Decisive when a situation demands fast action; able to juggle multiple demands at once; often energetic and resilient.

+     Likely to be described by others as having lively, fun, colorful personalities.

## Potential shortcomings

-     Not particularly reflective nor are they inclined to consider the past as a solid guide for the future. Thus, they may repeat some mistakes; display limited self-insight and can overrate their positive qualities and abilities.

-     Shift gears quickly, can get too many things going on at once, overly optimistic about what they or others can accomplish in a given period of time; weak handling administrative duties.

-     Interest in a project diminishes considerably at the tail end or when they fall into a routine. Then they can leave projects in disarray as they move on to other, more interesting pursuits.

-     Can be hasty and impulsive decision makers; oftentimes, they catch trends early, but go with *fads* too readily and eagerly.

-     There can be a clear element of oversell to their interpersonal style, which will be a turn off to people who are down-to-earth or street smart.

- Difficulty grasping technical information because they are impatient, not necessarily because they lack intelligence.
- Likely to be weak handling precise work or that requiring indepth, review and analysis.
- Occasionally, say things without thinking them through, (i.e., put their foot in their mouths).
- Procrastinate in areas they find unenjoyable and their follow through can be inconsistent.
- As managers, they expect too much of others as a result of overestimating their abilities and underestimating their limitations; likely to offer too much autonomy and freedom to their personnel.
- First impressions, good or bad, can carry too much weight with them.

## Other attributes

* Comfortable in a leadership position; readily delegate responsibility, strive to fully utilize the talent of their team; can be inspiring leaders.
* Can be highly instinctive decision makers and intuitive in approach to relationships.
* Need an environment where there is continual change, stimulation, freedom from tight supervision, room for innovation; want to work with high energy, creative, dynamic people.
* Willing to act on their creative impulses, which can be both good and bad. When operating within their area of skill or expertise, things can work out well, but not so if they are in an unfamiliar area.

## Incompatible pairing

The opposite of the Artistic / Enterprising combination is the Conventional / Investigative (or reverse) pair.

AEs find the rule-bound tendencies of CIs when making decisions incomprehensible. For their part, AEs do not hesitate to bend the rules or dispense with them altogether if they feel it necessary *or interesting* to do so. AEs thoroughly enjoy experimenting, pursuing innovative ideas and exploring their imagination. If AEs are managers of CIs, the latter will find such an approach to running a department or directing projects stressful. If CIs and AEs are coworkers, AEs will tend to dominate because they are assertive, despite the fact CIs on the team will likely have better insight into the technical aspects of important decisions being made. Also in this regard, AEs are mainly forward looking when making decisions, but not inclined to carefully consider past practice or established precedents, which CIs respect. AEs can dominate and intimidate CIs because they are expressive and unafraid to speak their minds. This can result in good ideas of CIs being overridden.

## Illustrative occupations

AE    Floral salesperson
EA    Public relations representative

## Illustrative interests

AE    Choral singing, fiction writing
EA    Clowning (performing)

## Potentially extreme behaviors

The following is a brief discussion of behavior this pair *could* exhibit under highly stressful or difficult situations or as a result of allowing certain attributes to develop to an extreme. It should be noted that these behaviors are rarely apt to be exhibited and most people described by this pair of Holland themes will *never* exhibit them. This discussion is included to convey a deeper sense of the range of qualities each pair could display. By talking about extremes, it is possible to further illuminate typical behaviors, attributes, et cetera.

The AEs high energy, spontaneity and readiness to take risks can work against them. They can make important decisions too quickly and without considering enough data thereby, opening the door to potential disaster. Similarly, AEs can jump into personal or business relationships without carefully sizing up the other person(s) involved. Furthermore, because of their persuasiveness and tendency to quickly seize new ideas, AEs can effectively sell others on a flawed idea without realizing the inherent risks that exist or to what degree. The disarray AEs sometimes leave behind on projects that have lost their interest can create extreme organizational or administrative difficulties for others to sort through and resolve.

# CHAPTER 19

◆

# ARTISTIC-CONVENTIONAL TYPES: INHIBITED

**Potential strengths**

+   Quiet, amiable, courteous people who demonstrate restraint and control over their emotions.

+   They can be imaginative within well-defined boundaries that reflect their particular areas of interest.

+   While not wildly creative themselves, they are certainly capable of taking others' creative ideas and extending or building upon them.

+   Their work is likely to be precise and tightly controlled; it is also apt to be appealing if not completely original.

+   They keep close tabs on tasks and assignments they are responsible for completing. They are effective following through on important duties or obligations; demonstrate patience when handling tedious, detailed assignments.

+ Generally well organized and orderly achieving results; tend to develop a set way of doing things as well as careful routines.
+ Hold themselves to high, sometimes exacting standards.
+ They follow rules, policies and established standards; respect authority and are normally deferential or compliant in subordinate roles. Nevertheless, apt to be inwardly critical of superiors who do not measure up to their standards.
+ Demonstrate quiet persistence in getting things done; work steadily and without fanfare.
+ Capable of seeing the practical side of issues or problems; avoid taking needless chances; prefer to err on the side of conservatism and caution.
+ Have the potential to do an effective job handling administrative responsibilities so long as this does not represent the majority of their work. Despite this, they may not really enjoy such work.

## Potential shortcomings

- Become frustrated and self-critical if they do not measure up to their, sometimes lofty standards or those of people important to them.
- When upset or angry, likely to suffer in silence and keep their feelings inside; despite this, others will strongly suspect they are unhappy.
- Unassertive, avoid conflict or controversy even if they hold strong opinions; yet, can be quietly critical of others whom they do not respect or with whom they disagree.
- Can feel considerable inner tension, anxiety as a result of the "psychic" clash between their strong need for control and desire to be creative and flexible.

- May become too caught up in doing things "properly" and within well-defined parameters; reluctant to cut corners or make exceptions to the rules even when appropriate.
- Their tendency to hold in feelings—especially negative ones—can result in such feelings building up over time. When the final straw has broken the camel's back, they can become unreasonable or emotional and may convey such feelings through sarcasm.
- They can be passively aggressive or quietly resistive handling disagreements or managing relationships with people they do not like nor respect.
- Steer away from bold, bright or flamboyant ideas, preferring to tone them down so as not to draw undue attention to themselves. They tend to be too conforming versus free-thinking.
- Their good ideas can be overlooked because they are reluctant to say what they think in a forthright, direct fashion.
- Sensitive to criticism of their work, ideas, performance, they take such comments personally.

## Other attributes

* Work best when their role is clear and there are well-established guidelines to follow; prefer a predictable environment that is not fast paced or variable from day to day; not likely to operate effectively in a pressure-filled, tense environment.
* Do not aspire to leadership positions, but aim to become highly competent within their role or area of expertise.
* Recognition for a job well done and their contributions is well-appreciated.
* They have an interest in cultural matters and can exhibit a refined, yet conservative outlook or orientation.

## Sources of conflict or tension for AC or CA pairs

The Artistic-Conventional pair is one of three unique combinations (the others being Realistic-Social and Investigative-Enterprising) in the Holland scheme. If you recall earlier in the text, this pair sits opposite each other on the Holland hexagon, which means they are theoretic as well as true opposites in the Holland typology.

In practical terms this means individuals who are described by the AC, RS or IE pairs are likely to feel occasional tension, confusion, frustration or anxiety because of the values or needs clashes flowing from the differences in these themes. These feelings are likely to be felt more often if a person's first two theme scores are noticeably higher compared to their third theme score. The reason for this, is that in such cases, the individual is best described by the first two themes with considerably less influence coming from the other themes. Therefore, any moderating effect the third theme (or other themes) might have is significantly reduced.

This is not to suggest AC (or RS or IE) pairs are destined for lives of anxiousness. In reality, the intrapersonal conflict these individuals may experience can be used constructively and channeled, so that their lives become satisfying. In fact, the resolution of these conflicts can result in AC type being open-minded, flexible and balanced in many respects. The key is for these individuals to recognize and understand the nature of these differences and use them to their full benefit.

There are several bases for potential conflict within the Artistic / Conventional dyads. First of all, Cs are conservative in their outlook and are hesitant to change or try new ideas. As thrive on being imaginative, even challenging conventional thinking or ideas. They welcome innovation and enjoy change. Thus, while Cs prefer to follow systems or rules that have been developed and proven, As want to alter them, make exceptions and try ideas that are wholly new and different. As encourage experimentation and trial and error, while Cs do not want to take unnecessary chances.

Secondly, Cs are concerned with details, precision and rules. They prefer structure and predictability in their work and environment. As can lose track of or overlook details—especially those they find uninteresting or mundane. They often operate spontaneously or impulsively which can make staying organized a problem. As abhor routine, structure and a set way of doing things. While Cs can be impressive in their ability to effectively handle repetitive day-to-day duties, As lose interest in these quickly. The patience Cs display managing details and tedious assignments tend to confound As who find such work restrictive and confining.

Thirdly, Cs are emotionally controlled and restrained. They tend to keep their feelings in check. Thus, Cs are rarely open sharing how they feel or think. As can be moody and temperamental. Oftentimes, when they are "up" it shows and vice versa. In a group comprised of As and Cs, the As would become frustrated with the Cs inability to discuss their feelings and ideas freely. The Cs, on the other hand, would be uncomfortable with the "emotive-ness" of As and their lack of restraint and control over their feelings.

Fourthly, Cs are diligent, conscientious and practical in their work orientation. They make decisions and achieve goals in an orderly, systematic fashion. As are idealistic in their orientation and can demonstrate considerable variability in their work approach. At times, they can work long hours and demonstrate impressive focus attempting to achieve a valued goal. At other times, As can have difficulty focusing on a single priority for long and become scattered. In their way of thinking, As consider possibilities without reference to or concern for their viability, utility or reasonableness. Cs always evaluate their ideas from a practical, pragmatic perspective. Where As see potential, Cs see potential problems to overcome or avoid.

Finally, Cs enjoy working with things. They like to organize, track, count, measure, calculate and plan. As enjoy working with ideas. They prefer to think, invent, create, conceptualize and imagine. Generally speaking, Cs demonstrate strong numerical skills while As are, more often than not, deficient in this area.

The above differences between As and Cs are not a complete list, but do point out some major potential sources of intrapersonal conflict for people represented by the AC dyad. These are differences or issues that such individuals need to be aware of and address in a constructive fashion as any of these issues—in and of themselves—can cause considerable anxiety and even lead to interpersonal or work and career dissatisfaction.

It should also be noted that the spread of scores among a person's first three themes, from the highest to the lowest, will speak directly to the potential for conflict as noted earlier. For example, if the A and C scores are close and the third theme is significantly different (lower), the above conflicts (one or more) are apt to be present and felt more intensely by such individuals. Conversely, if a person's first three theme scores are close to each other, the conflict is less likely and, where present, felt less strongly. This is a result of the moderating or attenuating influence the third theme can impart.

## Illustrative occupations

AC / CA        Graphologist

## Illustrative interests

AC      Fiction reading
CA      Collecting glass paperweights

## Potentially extreme behavior

The following is a brief discussion of behavior this pair *could* exhibit under highly stressful or difficult situations or as a result of allowing certain attributes to develop to an extreme. It should be noted that these behaviors are rarely apt to be exhibited and most people described by this pair of Holland themes will *never* exhibit them. This discussion is included to convey a deeper sense of the range of qualities each pair could display. By talking about extremes, it is possible to further illuminate typical behaviors, attributes, et cetera.

ACs can waste an awful lot of energy controlling and suppressing their feelings and emotions. This can lead to repression or denial of them and the consequent heightened anxiety that often follows. It can also lead to considerable tension within relationships, as ACs may not be sufficiently open, venturesome and forthright. Furthermore, the need for control is their "demon" insofar as their creative, expressive sides are concerned. This quality can keep them from being spontaneous, bold and truly imaginative, taking risks, et cetera. Most unfortunate is that ACs can be extremely self-critical for not doing these things. This can truly become a frustrating and negative spiral for them. Thus, it is imperative that CAs come to understand these opposite elements of their mental makeup, and see to it the needs of each are satisfactorily met.

# Chapter 20

◆

# Social-Enterprising Types: People-oriented

## Potential strengths

+ Sociable, outgoing, verbally expressive; likely to have a ready sense of humor with an ability to laugh easily; strong social interaction skills with an ability to "read" people well; socially venturesome; the most outgoing, people-oriented of all pairs.

+ Can be warm and friendly as well as assertive and firm when necessary or a situation requires these qualities.

+ Able to balance a concern for achieving results with the needs of those they must depend upon to deliver those results; normally, they consider other's feelings when making decisions.

+ Both goal and people oriented; comfortable in a leadership role and managing others to achieve objectives; have high expectations of others yet, offer praise for a job well done.

+ Can be strategic especially in relations with others; politically astute and alert dealing with people; not easily taken advantage of.
+ Decisive when necessary, consider the effect of decisions on people and their reactions; able to see the long-range consequences of decisions; can be strategic in their thinking.
+ Not easily deterred from achieving their objectives; believe in their ability to overcome obstacles; have a competitive side.
+ Persuasive and engaging, even charming or charismatic; in an effort to win over others, they appeal to their needs; capable of overcoming other's objections.
+ Can be effective when making intuitive or instinctive decisions about people; good insight into people-related problems or issues.
+ Capable of picking up their pace as demands upon them begin to increase.
+ Enjoy coaching or teaching others to help them reach their full potential.

## Potential shortcomings

- Likely to be an element of over-sell to their self-presentation.
- Can be stubborn, especially when the attainment of a goal is jeopardized by others, or their mind is made up.
- Competitiveness can come out in a negative way when they strive to "outdo" others; coworkers may not be fully aware they are seen as competition.
- Can be quite political in their orientation at work. Their true intentions may not always be evident; others may sometimes feel manipulated by them, if only in an innocuous sort of way.
- When they feel frustrated or stymied by coworkers, can surprise them by being blunt and direct when airing their feelings once the final straw is reached.

- Their attention to detail and day-to-day concerns can vary considerably; tend to gloss over personally unimportant priorities, such as those of an administrative nature.
- Can talk or socialize too much on the job, distracting themselves and others from the work at hand.
- Do not always listen effectively, and can dominate meetings or discussions by talking at great length while being slow to make a point.
- They are not scientifically-minded nor technically-oriented; can oversimplify such problems.
- A need for recognition can result in their pursuing the limelight too often or readily.

## Other attributes

* Purposeful in relations with others.
* Their approach to planning tends to be broad based rather than meticulous.
* Comfortable in positions of authority and influence; enjoy the status of a visible leadership role.
* Prefer a competitive, but team-oriented environment where all are focused on achieving important goals. They expect rewards and recognition to flow from their accomplishments; are ambitious and want to advance their careers
* Strongly believe in their ability to "talk their way" through conflict and confrontations and are often able to do so.

## Incompatible pairing

The opposite combination of the Social / Enterprising is the Realistic / Investigative (or reverse) pair.

The potential for each to be stubborn can lead to difficult situations for both pairs. The RI may be quietly resistant rather than blatantly so (especially if the RI is in a subordinate role), which can further aggravate the SE who would prefer to discuss differences directly. In addition, RIs can be logical and systematic in their approach to doing things. This can be frustrating to SEs who may want to proceed in a flexible manner or follow their hunches or intuitions. The SE is the most people-oriented of the fifteen pairs, and the RI is one of the least people-oriented or sociable. This can lead to misunderstandings on the part of SEs who may interpret the RIs preference for limited contact as aloofness. The SEs desire to be decisive can conflict with the RIs desire to be careful and methodical. There are times when SEs will expect their ideas or accomplishments to be applauded, and will find RIs lack of acknowledgement upsetting.

## Illustrative occupations

SE    Hospital administrator
ES    Political scientist

## Illustrative interests

SE    Fund-raising, golf, foreign travel
ES    Business advising (volunteer), elected civic office

## Potentially extreme behavior

The following is a brief discussion of behavior this pair *could* exhibit under highly stressful or difficult situations or as a result of allowing certain attributes to develop to an extreme. It should be noted that these behaviors are rarely apt to be exhibited and most people described by this pair of Holland themes will *never* exhibit them. This discussion is included to convey a deeper sense of the range of qualities each pair could display. By talking about extremes, it is possible to further illuminate typical behaviors, attributes, et cetera.

SEs can focus so much energy outward (i.e., *toward* others) that they can lose sight of themselves, who they are and what they are about. SEs can sometimes be manipulative. That is, they may use their strong inter-personal and persuasive skills to take advantage of others. Moreover, the SE can be very political in their orientation at work, but also change their decisions or beliefs to suit their goals or to be in accord with prevailing opinion. Along these same lines, SEs may take too much of an interest in other's affairs, resulting in their being "gossipy." Beyond this, SEs are sometimes inclined to talk or try to manipulate their way out of difficul-ties, rather than facing them openly and honestly. Furthermore, while SEs surely enjoy the limelight—receiving accolades and recognition—they can be *manipulated* by others who are aware of this.

# CHAPTER 21

# SOCIAL-CONVENTIONAL TYPES: UNASSERTIVE

## Potential strengths

+ Easygoing, kindly, polite, helpful; unassuming and unpretentious in relations with others.

+ Soft spoken and low keyed; go along with the ideas of others so long as they are in line with their values and sense of right and wrong; work cooperatively with coworkers.

+ Careful with details because they are patient and methodical getting their work completed; recheck their work to avoid errors, mistakes.

+ Responsive to the needs of others; respect the authority and decisions of superiors; dutiful, compliant individuals.

+ They work quietly and without fanfare to achieve expected results; modest about their accomplishments or talents.

+ Work well within established rules, policies and procedures; unlikely to question or challenge these.

+ Conscientious and reliable; work steadily to complete assignments; deliver a predictable level of performance.

+ As managers, they are tolerant of others; quietly encouraging and supportive; offer credit for a job well done.

+ Tend not to become overly anxious when working under pressure, but normally remain even keeled during difficult times.

+ They want to do well no matter the assignment they undertake, and strive to do right by others.

+ Patient when handling slow moving, detailed or tedious assignments. They do a good job handling administrative duties.

+ Avoid making rash or impulsive decisions especially when others will be affected by their actions.

+ Dutiful, responsive and compliant; they readily follow the lead of their manager.

## Potential shortcomings

- Apt to assume more than their fair share of the work, and receive less than their fair share of the credit. Their needs can be overlooked because they do not call attention to themselves.

- Unassertive and timid; avoid disagreements, conflict, confrontations. Their unassuming, trusting nature can be taken advantage of by others.

- When upset, tend to keep to themselves; may suffer silently and retreat from others until they sort things through. They are sensitive to criticism and take it much too personally.

- Reluctant to criticize, reprimand or discipline others when such actions are deserved; too concerned with what others think of them, and do not want to risk offending or hurting others' feelings.

- Too self-critical, they fail to give themselves enough credit. In this regard, they can be their own worst enemies.

- Put off tough decisions that could meet with resistance or stir up controversy; self-doubts surface if their ideas are challenged by others; sometimes too concerned with making a mistake or doing the wrong thing.
- Intimidated by strong, forceful, aggressive individuals or authority figures; tend to be too deferential or submissive.
- Shy away from leadership roles. They lack confidence in their ability to lead.
- Adhere too closely to rules; afraid to make exceptions even if appropriate; avoid taking risks.
- May not possess a deep well of energy and stamina when working under stress and pressure, and demands increase significantly.
- Can display perfectionist tendencies, resulting in over working less critical tasks.
- Lack creativity and may question their "inspirations," instincts or intuition.

## Other attributes

* Prefer jobs where roles, procedures and guidelines are clear.
* Work well in a stable, relaxed environment where coworkers are friendly and conscientious; work best for a considerate, supportive and nurturing boss and someone who readily offers praise for a job well done.
* It would be especially stressful for them to work in a competitive, fast-paced environment because of their cooperative, helpful, easy-going nature.
* They can be quietly enthusiastic on the job, but keep such feelings inside until they are comfortable with coworkers and their surroundings.

## Incompatible pairing

The opposite of the Social / Conventional combination is the Realistic / Artistic (or reverse) pair.

It is fair, not merely coincidental, to say SCs carefully adhere to social conventions. Thus, they not only believe in the necessity of following work-related rules and procedures, but also those governing people's conduct and behavior. Consequently, SCs frown upon RAs for sometimes being indiscrete in what they have to say, or occasionally using humor that is too "earthy" or impolite. SCs are much concerned with propriety and doing what is right or correct in all instances, whereas RAs occasionally act in a manner SCs feel is inappropriate. SCs can also be too strict defining other's roles such that they can place restrictions on RAs activities that do not fully utilize their abilities. SCs caution, and perfectionist leanings, can clash with RAs willingness to sometimes do just what is necessary to complete an assignment without wasting time going beyond this.

## Illustrative occupations

SC     Medical assistant
CS     Financial analyst

## Illustrative interests

SC     Teaching aide
CS     Collecting baseball cards

## Potentially extreme behavior

The following is a brief discussion of behavior this pair *could* exhibit under highly stressful or difficult situations or as a result of allowing certain attributes to develop to an extreme. It should be noted that these behaviors are rarely apt to be exhibited and most people described by this pair of Holland themes will *never* exhibit them. This discussion is included to convey a deeper sense of the range of qualities each pair could display. By talking about extremes, it is possible to further illuminate typical behaviors, attributes, et cetera.

The emotional and other needs of SCs can easily be overlooked because they do not speak up enough for themselves, nor do they go after what they require. Similarly, they can end up passed over for opportunities on the job because they call little attention to themselves, their accomplishments or aspirations. In fact, SCs may allow others to take credit for things they have done. Negative situations can be allowed by SCs to go on too long before they take any action to remedy them. Moreover, the reluctance of SCs to take risks can cause them to lose out on some wonderful opportunities. SCs may have problems related to a lack of self-esteem or a weak self-image. Fear of failure, making mistakes or letting someone down, can substantially limit their willingness to take risks—curtailing personal and professional development.

# CHAPTER 22

◆

# ENTERPRISING-CONVENTIONAL TYPES: BUSINESS-MINDED

## Potential strengths

+    Tend to achieve their objectives in a systematic, orderly fashion; set their sights high and display determination working toward objectives.

+    Possess a sense of urgency; yet, will not hurry needlessly or cut corners at the expense of accuracy.

+    Develop clear goals and the plans necessary to achieve them; delegate responsibility as necessary and proscribed by established roles.

+    Can be effective administrative supervisors or managers who establish definite rules and procedures for guiding the work being done; establish challenging goals for others to achieve.

+     Generally, stick to proven methods, but will take risks within well-defined areas where the cost of an error would be minimal or controllable. They are not reckless risk takers.

+     Willing to express their displeasure or disagreement when they are unhappy with results or see things differently from others.

+     Maintain control over work they are responsible for completing or have delegated to others.

+     They have the potential to understand the big picture *and* how the details must fit together to complete it. Similarly, able to take account of both the strategic and tactical implications of their decisions.

+     The most business minded of all pairs. They have a keen concern for the bottom-line and are mindful of costs associated with their decisions; always striving to maximize profits.

+     They are purposeful and take their jobs seriously. They are also ambitious and career oriented.

## Potential shortcomings

-     Can be too exacting in their standards, and find imprecision in others' work frustrating.

-     As supervisors, they can exert too much control over the work of associates; inclined to supervise too closely if they question a person's ability to be thorough; may fail to delegate enough responsibility *and* authority to team members. They can hold onto responsibilities they should turn over to others.

-     When criticizing others' work or performance, can be unsympathetic regarding extenuating circumstances and too pointed with their comments. As managers, can fail to offer enough praise and encouragement.

-   In relations with others, can sometimes be too direct expressing their opinions and insufficiently understanding or tolerant of divergent views.
-   Unyielding in certain areas, particularly with respect to established rules, procedures, guidelines and expectations.
-   Sometimes exhibit a strong tendency to press hard for their own views, ideas over those of others. This reflects competitiveness and a fairly strong need for control.
-   May fail to be flexible enough in their outlook; hesitant to change their plans or decisions once they are set in motion.
-   At times, they can focus too much on short-term problems and issues. At other times, they can focus too much on long-term problems and issues; either can occur when they become immersed in particular matters that capture their interest.
-   Some may present their accomplishments, ideas or selves in an overly favorable light.

## Other attributes

*   Can come across as reserved and deferential or outgoing and assertive—depending upon whom they are dealing with and the nature of the situation. The former can occur when they relate to personnel higher in the management hierarchy, and the latter when dealing with peers or those seen as lower on the management hierarchy.
*   Often ambitious and want to have more authority, control and influence, especially over areas where they have expertise or experience.
*   Prefer goal-oriented environments where people are conscientious, self-motivated, can operate somewhat independently, and where there is a clear career track.

*    Not well suited for working in or managing a research-oriented or scientific department because they are too bottom-line focused. They are well-suited to managing in a structured organization with a clear hierarchy, such as an accounting or law firm.

## Incompatible pairing

The opposite combination of the Enterprising / Conventional is the Investigative / Artistic (or reverse) pair.

The EC, with their need for control, can be frustrated by the independent minded and free thinking IAs. Conversely, the IA is apt to resent the ECs desire for control. In addition, the sometimes unyielding nature of ECs can be upset by the IAs flexible style. When an IA sees a logical reason for doing things differently from established rules, the EC may interpret their behavior as insubordination or a lack of respect. The EC may see the IAs desire to thoroughly explore an interesting idea in depth as a waste of precious time or resources. ECs can tend to view IAs as lacking a practical or "business sense." Finally, ECs focus so much on organizational goals that they can lose sight of the needs and interests of employees working for the organization.

## Illustrative occupations

EC    County auditor
CE    Senior budget analyst

## Illustrative interests

EC    Stock market investing, commodities trading
CE    Collecting antiques, tax preparation, computer chess

## Potentially extreme behavior

The following is a brief discussion of behavior this pair *could* exhibit under highly stressful or difficult situations or as a result of allowing certain attributes to develop to an extreme. It should be noted that these behaviors are rarely apt to be exhibited and most people described by this pair of Holland themes will *never* exhibit them. This discussion is included to convey a deeper sense of the range of qualities each pair could display. By talking about extremes, it is possible to further illuminate typical behaviors, attributes, et cetera.

ECs can be overly controlling in relationships to the point where they may stifle others' growth. In this regard, they are inclined to narrowly define other's roles in personal and work relationships. They may also establish impossibly high standards for themselves and others, leading to tremendous frustration and anxiety for all parties concerned, especially when goals are not reached. ECs can be so ambitious and career-oriented that they focus too much on that aspect of their lives to the detriment of other areas. Likewise, they can be intolerant of people at work who do not display their level of ambition and commitment, despite the fact those individuals may well be fine employees in other important regards. ECs can be hierarchical in their outlook as managers, thereby establishing a restrictive set of roles for people on their team to fit into.

# CHAPTER 23

# DEVELOPING YOUR OWN PERSONAL PROFILE

This chapter will guide you through a number of exercises to aid in developing your  personal profile based upon information presented in chapters 1 through 6 and chapters 8 through 22. The first three exercises are based upon your results from the self-tests at the end of chapters 1 through 6. If you have not yet completed these self-tests, do so now and return to this chapter.

Complete the following exercises according to the instructions provided. Read through them carefully.

## Exercise 1: Making sense of your highest Holland-theme score.

### Step One

My highest Holland score from the self-tests is for the: _____ theme. (If two scores tied for the highest, select the one that comes up first in the word, RIASEC.)

My raw score on this theme is: _____

This raw score translates into the: _____ percentile range (See chapter 7).

### Step Two

Refer to the chapter where your highest theme score is described. Read through the entire description.

### Step Three

Re-read the same section of the chapter from step two above. But, this time, as you read, highlight, underline or otherwise note, those parts of the description you feel can or do apply to you.

### Step Four

In the space provided, write down the descriptions of your highest Holland score you indicated as descriptive of yourself (i.e., highlighted sections).
Write this information under the appropriate heading corresponding to the chapter 1 through 6 headings.

Interpersonal style

Talents, abilities and decision making

Work style and motivational factors

Leadership

Interests: occupational and academic

Exercise 2a: Making sense of your *second* highest Holland-theme score.

*Step One*

My second highest Holland score on the self-test is for the: _____ theme. (If two scores were tied for the highest or second highest, enter the one that comes up next in the word, RIASEC.)

My raw score on this theme is: _____

This raw score translates into the: _____ percentile range (See chapter 7).

*Step Two*

Refer to the section of chapters 1 through 6 where your second-highest theme is described. Read through the entire description.

*Step Three*

Re-read the same section of chapters 1 through 6 noted above. But, this time, as you read, highlight, underline or otherwise note, those parts of the description you feel can or do apply to you.

*Step Four*

In the space provided, write down the descriptions of your second highest Holland score, which you indicated as descriptive of yourself. Write this information under the appropriate headings corresponding to the chapters 1 through 6 headings.

Interpersonal style

Talents, abilities and decision making

Work style and motivational factors

Leadership

Interests: occupational and academic

<u>Exercise 2b: Making sense of your *second* highest Holland-theme score.</u>
(Complete this exercise only if you had a tie for your highest or second highest Holland-theme score.)

## *Step One*

My second highest Holland score on the self-test is for the: _____ theme. (If two scores were tied for the highest or second highest, enter the one that came up next in the word, RIASEC.)

My raw score on this theme is: _____

This raw score translates into the: _____ percentile range (See chapter 7).

## *Step Two*

Refer to the section of chapters 1 through 6 where your second-highest theme is described. Read through the entire description.

## *Step Three*

Re-read the same section of chapters 1 through 6. But, this time, as you read, highlight, underline or otherwise note, those parts of the description you feel can or do apply to you.

## *Step Four*

In the space provided, write down the descriptions of your second-highest Holland score, which you indicated as descriptive of yourself. Write this information under the appropriate headings corresponding to the chapters 1 through 6 headings.

Interpersonal style

Talents, abilities and decision making

Work style and motivational factors

Leadership

Interests: occupational and academic

Exercise 3: Making sense of the combination of your two highest Holland-theme scores (e.g., pairs).

*Step One*

My two highest Holland scores from the self-tests were for the:_____ theme and _____ theme.

*Step Two*

Refer to the section of chapters 8 through 22 where the above *pair* of Holland themes is described. If you do not find this ordering, look up the *reverse* ordering of your two highest themes. Read through the entire description.

*Step Three*

Re-read the same section of chapters 8 through 22. But, this time, as you read, highlight, underline or otherwise note, those parts of the description that you feel can or do apply to you.

*Step Four*

In the space provided below, write down the descriptions of your Holland pair, which you indicated as descriptive of yourself. Write this information under the appropriate heading that corresponds with the chapter 8 through 22 headings.

**Potential Strengths**

**Potential Shortcomings**

**Other Attributes**

## Exercise 4: Putting it all together.

### *Step One*

Refer back to all of the information you wrote down for exercises 1 through 3. In the left- hand margin, or next to where you wrote each statement, use the following rating scale to determine which of the statements you wrote down *best define* you:

| Rating | Meaning |
|--------|---------|
| 1 | I am *absolutely certain* I am well described by this statement or adjective. |
| 2 | In *many circumstances*, but, not always, I can be described in this way. |
| 3 | I am *not completely sure* this statement or adjective is accurate of me. |

## *Step Two*

Below, write down all of the statements or adjectives you rated as a 1 or 2 under the appropriate heading.

I view the following as my Key Strengths:

I view the following as my Developmental Areas or areas to work on:

Exercise 5: Utilizing feedback from others.

Oftentimes, it is useful to cross-validate our self-opinions against the opinions of others who know us well. Have someone you know and trust, and who knows you well, read the sections of chapters 1 through 6 and 8 through 22 you referred to in completing exercises 1 through 3. Ask them to read the Personal Profile you developed for yourself in exercise 4. Based upon their comments, add or delete statements to/from your profile. In this way, you can better ensure you have accurately described your strengths and developmental areas. As you pursue your job search, use the information you have gained through this process to improve the match between your strengths, capabilities, work style, et cetera, and the openings you learn about.

---◆---

# DISCOVERING WHERE YOU WILL BE HAPPY

Part Three describes characteristics of the six Holland themes translated into work environments. Recall that the Holland theory is a theory of personality *and* environments. For each theme there is a corresponding environment that possesses certain identifiable attributes or characteristics. That is, a work (or other) setting where a group of people exists for some purpose, can be identified within the Holland scheme of things. These groups, if largely composed of people identified as one or another Holland theme, will tend to create environments consistent with the predominant theme.

Consequently, the different Holland environments will have dissimilar values, mores, expectations, et cetera, compared to each other. This is especially true of environments that are opposite each other in the hexagonal arrangement discussed in chapter 1 (e.g., R / S, I / E and A / C). It is also true that certain Holland environments are somewhat similar to each other and will share some common characteristics (e.g., R / I, I / A, A / S, S / E, E / C, C / R).

It should also be noted that just as people could be described in terms of their highest two or three Holland themes, so too can environments. A company or department within a company can be called an IAS environment, an IA, or any other such combination.

The above suggests that a certain synergy is established when a group of people who can be characterized by the same Holland theme(s) come together. This is basically correct. Like minds (or personalities in this case) will tend to produce an atmosphere or culture that is fairly homogenous and consistent with their shared values and principles. Such groups will possess certain strengths and excel in certain tasks, or work and operate in a reasonably predictable fashion—generally speaking. Conversely, these same groups will exhibit an aversion to certain tasks or work (or people) and possess certain shortcomings or limitations.

It can be valuable for people to assess work environments when searching for a job or considering accepting employment with a particular organization. The Realistic individual who is mulling over an offer of employment in a largely Social environment would spare themselves considerable anguish, frustration and disappointment by passing on the opportunity and continuing the job search. On the other hand, that same Realistic person may want to strongly consider accepting a job offer from a company that has a predominantly Investigative or Conventional environment. While there will be some trade- offs if they go with such an organization, they will also find a number of commonalities between their personality and the organizational culture that will be agreeable.

It can be invaluable for organizations to know how their environment would be described in Holland terms. For example, if a company knows it has an Enterprising / Conventional environment, it can better select people who will be compatible with it and who will have a greater likelihood of succeeding. Such an organization might want to avoid candidates who are highly Investigative or Artistic, as there would be many potential points of conflict for all parties concerned. By the same token, an EC company might want to introduce some individuals who are EAs or SCs as they could add some diversity to the organization and some fresh ideas or perspectives that might be lacking currently.

Knowing how a company's culture could be described in Holland terms can be instructive in identifying training programs it may want to introduce. This information can help management identify skills or abilities the organization may lack or possess in insufficient quantities. A Human Resource department would find this information helpful when it comes to recruiting and interviewing job candidates.

Obviously, there are many practical benefits to individuals and organizations who know and understand the Holland theory and how it can be applied.

◆

# CHAPTER 24

# REALISTIC ENVIRONMENTS: "CAN YOU GET THE JOB DONE?"

### What they are like

The Realistic environment possesses a good deal of structure. This will take shape in the form of clear goals, standards, expectations and role definitions. There is normally little in the way of ambiguity in Realistic environments because Realistic individuals find this attribute frustrating and discomforting. There is oftentimes a definite chain of command or pecking order in Realistic environments. In fact, the military model is a fine example of such an environment. So is a police department.

Realistic environments are characterized by predictability, consistency and traditional ways of doing things. People in these organizations usually resist change and prize tried- and-true methods or approaches over innovation. People in realistic environments normally aim for concrete goals that are tangible, quantitative and measurable. Frequently, there is a production component involved in the work undertaken with a definite focus on efficient use of time and resources.

Despite the structure inherent in Realistic environments, they are normally informal places to work where people relate to each other in a straightforward or no-nonsense-like fashion. There is a notable lack of pretense displayed by people in these environments. Yet, at the same time, Realistic environments are also places where workers are serious minded and task focused. In these environments, work comes before pleasure. In many cases, Realistic environments have a competitive tone. This can flow from the fact that productivity is often a means for gauging both an individual's and the group's performance, or simply from the fact R-types enjoy competition.

## Nature of the Work

Oftentimes, Realistic environments are production focused. As such, clear, concrete goals are the norm, and the means to achieve them are equally clear. The work usually requires the hands-on involvement of employees, and speed of results is important because everyone is usually working within established deadlines. Frequently, the work being done in a Realistic environment is mechanically oriented or technical, and personnel doing the work are expected to follow set procedures and guidelines without fail.

## What is rewarded?

Realistic environments value a sense of duty. Along with this, a deep feeling of responsibility towards coworkers and, more importantly, the organization, is reinforced. So, Realistic organizations expect loyalty and a sense of dedication from its workers. Respect for authority is considered crucial to achieving results and keeping order. Furthermore, there are likely to be a number of clearly established routines in Realistic environments; these are helpful in organizing everyone's efforts and activities.

Everyone in such environments is considered important *collectively,* as it is a group effort that is deemed critical to reaching overall objectives. Consequently, everyone is counted on to meet the requirements of their job in a reliable fashion, and clear lines of accountability are established.

Yet, self-reliance is equally valued in Realistic environments. It is expected that workers in such environments will learn their jobs well enough that they can perform effectively and dependably without tight supervision. They are also expected to know when to ask for help or direction while demonstrating initiative completing assignments.

Realistic environments oftentimes value an artisan-like work approach and seeing a job completed properly the first time. There is a pragmatic quality found in these environments or organizations and common sense is viewed as a definite virtue. However, personnel lacking these attributes will be looked upon unfavorably. It is frequently noted that people in Realistic environments display a "doer mentality." This translates into a preference to stay busy and active while on the job, and a desire on the part of workers to be hands-on, getting things done without a concern for getting dirty—literally, if necessary.

## Getting Ahead

Advancement in Realistic environments is earned through a number of means. One has to do with a person's "time in service." That is, tenure in a position or with the organization is frequently given considerable weight when reviewing people for advancement. A second important requirement for getting ahead in these environments is the level of skill or proficiency a worker displays in their current job. Oftentimes, the employees who have been promoted were the most productive or effective in a prior role compared to others. A third basis for moving people up in Realistic environments has to do with a person's respect for authority and established rules or standards. A fourth attribute important in advancing within such organizations has to do with a person's focus on their work compared to the amount of time they spend interacting with coworkers. Individuals who do not over-socialize and always complete their assignments, stand a better chance of moving up than do their very social coworkers. Finally, those who advance within Realistic organizations have demonstrated unquestionable loyalty.

## Pitfalls

Realistic environments tend not to be warm, supportive or nurturing. It is frequently true in such organizations that you will know you are doing well if no one tells you are not. Put another way, there is unlikely to be much praise or positive recognition offered in such environments. Yet, criticism is apt to be direct and to-the-point.

Because Realistic environments are task focused, there will be a lot of "work," but not much "play." This is not to suggest these environments are humorless or unenjoyable. However, in some cases the humor may seem coarse or too "earthy" for others. Some such organizations or departments within organizations that are Realistic-dominated, can develop an "us versus them" mentality with respect to other groups or areas inside or outside of the company. Acceptance of new members can be a slow process due to the inherent guardedness of such groups.

## Leadership

It should not be too surprising to find that Realistic environments can be (and often are) managed in a "top-down" fashion. That is, the person in charge is expected to establish a clear chain of command. As noted earlier, a military model is a good example of a Realistic environment. Thus, leadership tends to be crisp, direct and roles of all participants are well defined which helps to ensure little ambiguity exists. Leadership in Realistic environments can lean toward being rule-oriented and disciplinarian which results in a lack of tolerance for creative expression or experimentation. Such leaders will often encourage competition as a means to motivate their workers.

Leadership in Realistic environments is, essentially, non-democratic inasmuch as whomever is in charge expects compliance with their decisions without discussion, dissension or objection. There will be a lack of nurturing and positive feedback, and clear, direct criticism when things go wrong or production schedules are not met. Peer pressure is another method used by leaders in Realistic environments to gain conformity. In this regard, workers are encouraged to confront personnel who are not performing as expected or doing their jobs properly.

# CHAPTER 25

───────◆───────

# INVESTIGATIVE ENVIRONMENTS: "ARE YOU AN EXPERT?"

**What they are like**

The Investigative environment normally has limited structure and little in the form of hard-line rules, policies or procedures. Despite this, there *will be* clear standards with respect to the quality and integrity of everyone's work or particular formulas or methods for completing certain critical tasks.

Individuals within Investigative environments are typically given a good deal of autonomy and are expected to work well independently. Likewise, people in these environments are expected to be knowledgeable in a particular field or area of specialization. They must also know when a problem or issue lies outside their realm of expertise or training, and seek assistance from appropriate personnel in such instances. Workers in Investigative environments are unlikely to operate under close direction from a supervisor or manager—once their knowledge level or skills have been demonstrated.

There is frequently an air of professionalism found in Investigative environments. Coinciding with this, these environments are often relatively serious in tone, not particularly warm and somewhat formal, but also relaxed or calm. Consequently, humor is likely to be of the dry variety and outward expressions of excitement or enthusiasm tend to be muted or restrained. Flowing from the reserved nature of Investigative types, these environments can, to outsiders, appear somewhat impenetrable. That is, people working within Investigative environments do not readily extend themselves to others nor are they skilled networkers. As such, an Investigative department can be something of a "closed society" whose members interact with others on an as-necessary basis.

## Nature of the work

All Investigative environments are analytic in nature. That is, a significant portion of the work consists of gathering, reviewing, interpreting data and information as well as conducting research. Some Investigative environments focus on developing ideas that can lead to better products, services, processes, results, et cetera. In this sense, new ideas are valued within Investigative environments if they are logical and can stand up to close scrutiny and rigorous testing and analysis. When change is brought into Investigative organizations, it is introduced in a systematic, measured and planned fashion. Moreover, these environments are often scientifically- or technically-oriented (i.e., a research and development laboratory within a chemical company or a marketing research firm).

Goals within Investigate environments are apt to be broadly defined and even somewhat (or very) ambiguous. Since the work being done in these environments can, at times, be rather conceptual or theoretical in nature, this makes sense. Specific policies, systems or guidelines that are established will be determined on the basis of what is logical and rationale for a given department or operation.

## What is rewarded?

Investigative environments value intelligence, critical thinking, original ideas and sound logic. Curiosity and inquisitiveness are equally important. So too, is the ability to ask the "right" questions to resolve a problem, or at least frame it in a way that leads to an eventual solution. Because Investigative environments are analytical in nature, thorough research is viewed as essential to doing a good job with appropriate documentation of such research completed in detail.

Investigative environments prize strategic planning and intellectual agility. These two attributes require another, and that is the ability to not only see details, but how they must fit together—logically—to complete the larger picture. Expertness is another important value of Investigative environments.

The ability to discuss differences of opinion and to grasp and understand many different facets of an issue or problem is greatly valued in Investigative environments. In this area, diplomacy and tact are reinforced over confrontation and directness. In fact, the lack of directness among people in these environments can be frustrating to individuals from other areas of an organization.

Conscientiousness, discipline and patience in completing difficult tasks or assignments are all valued qualities in Investigative environments. On the other hand, a keen sense of urgency that could result in haste or impulsive decisions is frowned upon even if the end results are acceptable. Investigative environments are not characterized by a lot of socializing or small talk among coworkers, except when it revolves around the work itself or, importantly, intriguing ideas. Oddly, while Investigative environments are not competitive by nature, competition among different or opposing ideas, theories or conceptual frameworks *can exist*.

## Getting Ahead

Advancement in Investigative environments is earned through a number of means. One has to do with a person's accumulated knowledge and technical expertise. Thus, in such organizations, what you know and how thoroughly you know it is a true source of power and influence. A second important requirement for getting ahead revolves around an individual's problem solving or analytical skills. Those who have a strong critical thinking ability will be looked upon favorably when opportunities to take on added responsibilities arise, especially when those responsibilities involve handling and resolving an important organizational problem. A third factor that comes into play in moving ahead in Investigative environments involves a person's skill in thinking strategically and knowing when to introduce change and innovation. This includes the ability to periodically generate new ideas. A fourth basis for advancing in Investigative environments has to do with a person's breadth of understanding of such organizations' operations, systems, strengths, weaknesses and other such critical factors.

## Pitfalls

Certain Investigative environments can seen cool or impersonal, as there is little emphasis on such things as people's feelings or emotions. Neither do these environments encourage much expressiveness, let alone assertiveness. In addition, the focus on strict logic can eliminate the possibility of valuable, but intuitively-generated ideas gaining support. Related to this, Investigative environments can fail to take enough risks, as there is a propensity in such organizations to undertake considerable research and testing before new ideas are introduced.

Investigative environments can be critical environments given that the key element of analytical thought is examining the flaws of an idea thoroughly. Such critical review can leave some people feeling offended when their suggestions are debated and discarded. Within Investigative environments, there may not be sufficient action; instead, there can be too much of a propensity to discuss ideas or decisions, which can slow down the process of getting things accomplished. Moreover, it can be a gradual process for a new person in an Investigative environment to gain coworkers respect. It must be earned by proving that your knowledge, skills and abilities are on par with everyone else.

## Leadership

One key basis for achieving a leadership role in Investigative environments is possession of relevant expertise in a given area critical to the success of the organization or department. So too, is the ability to grasp the bigger picture and understand the strategic implications of important decisions. Leaders of such environments normally provide their personnel broad, overall objectives, with room for the individual to determine the details or formulate relevant sub-goals.

Roles for personnel in Investigative environments are defined along the lines of the requirements of specific projects they are working on, and the knowledge and expertise each possesses. Within the realm of a person's expertise, they are often given considerable latitude to perform their jobs, so long as they are rigorous in their methodologies and conscientious achieving objectives.

It is unlikely leaders within Investigative environments will provide much in the way of positive recognition because the nature of the work being done, problems addressed and knowledge gained are expected to be self-rewarding. Nevertheless, such leaders are apt to be fair-handed, reasonably democratic, and open to considering the merits of opposing ideas that have a sound, logical foundation. In fact, discussions of this sort are often encouraged. Conversely, Investigative leaders can be dismissive regarding ideas or views they feel lack clear, factual support.

An area that can be lax in Investigative environments has to do with handling performance and personnel problems. This flows from the fact that Investigative types are indirect, unassertive and non-confrontive by nature. As a result, these types of matters can go on too long before being addressed in such environments.

# CHAPTER 26

# ARTISTIC ENVIRONMENTS: "ARE YOU CREATIVE?"

**What they are like**

The Artistic environment is loosely structured or, unstructured. Generally, there are no hard and fast rules; those that exist are frequently looked upon as flexible *guidelines* that are open to interpretation or subject to change. Goals and expectations in Artistic environments are relatively vague, general or ambiguous. For example, one goal could be to come up with imaginative and creative ideas quickly. How this would occur would be left up to the individual.

Artistic environments can be very fast-changing environments, and are not characteristically, highly predictable from week-to-week or year-to-year. This tends to generate an air of anticipation and excitement— or, anxiety and tension, depending upon a person's particular Holland orientation. Because ideas can flow and be discussed readily in Artistic environments, brainstorming sessions can be lively, free-wheeling discussions. In Artistic environments, off-the-wall, unusual and, otherwise different ideas, thoughts and methods are acceptable. Thus, spontaneity, expressiveness and a lack of inhibition are not frowned upon by coworkers.

Oftentimes, Artistic environments are informal organizations where people's personalities and tastes are readily evident in their office decor, demeanor and work styles. New projects are frequently greeted with great interest while routine, recurring responsibilities are viewed as tedious and put off if at all possible. There is likely to be a rather relaxed approach to managing people in Artistic organizations.

Due to the intense personal nature of the creative process, Artistic environments can produce volatile atmospheres where emotions and feelings can come to a boil suddenly, or with seemingly little provocation.

## Nature of the work

A definite emphasis is placed on creativity and imagination in Artistic environments. Novel, fresh, odd, unusual or non-traditional ideas and approaches are encouraged. The work being done is expected to be expressive and original, as well as innovative. It can be completed independently or in teams, whichever method is preferred, and yields creative results. Oftentimes, work in Artistic environments is project based (e.g., developing a new greeting card line or illustrating a book). The work being done can be hands-on and concrete (e.g., creating a model for a new product idea), or conceptual (e.g., coming up with lyrics and music for a television ad campaign). Rules governing how work is to be done are either loosely defined, developed along the way, or spontaneously created as necessary. In many instances, workers in Artistic environments are working under the pressure of deadlines—which are often pushed. To outsiders, these environments can appear disorderly or unorganized, but people working within them would argue they have their own *unique* organizational methods. Those methods, however, will unlikely follow normal, logical principles, since logic or rational thinking can interfere with creative thinking.

## What is rewarded?

Artistic environments value imaginative thinking, change and innovation. If individuals in such environments can produce fresh, creative ideas, many of their own shortcomings can be tolerated. The quality of a person's ideas and end results is also important. Intertwined with these attributes, autonomy and freedom from certain organizational restrictions are frequently an unspoken reward for solid performance. Consequently, strict adherence to standard operating procedures is not reinforced as a job requirement.

While autonomy is often provided, the ability to work effectively with other team members to complete a project is a necessity. This requires workers in Artistic environments be able to set aside their own personal preferences or biases. At times, that can be difficult if it means one person's ideas are deemed more creative or desirable than another's. So, there can be a tense, inter-dependence coexisting alongside the freedom of an Artistic environment.

Artistic environments reinforce adaptability and resourcefulness in meeting the organizations needs and demands. Taking risks is certainly a key element in Artistic environments, and the willingness to do so—successfully—can be well rewarded. An additional quality that is looked upon favorably, is the ability to generate many potentially usable or saleable ideas quickly.

## Getting Ahead

Advancement in Artistic environments is earned through a number of means. One has to do with simply being creative and, importantly, creative *and* successfully so over a long period of time. A second basis for moving ahead in Artistic environments has to do with being consistent, reliable and timely in completing projects. This is important because Artistic types can frequently be challenged in these areas. A third critical requirement for moving up in Artistic environments has to do with a person's ability to take ideas or goals that are ambiguous or loosely defined and turn them into something that is concrete, tangible and practical. A fourth valuable attribute involves being able to operate effectively in a changeable, unpredictable environment, and provide direction to others. Finally, those who advance within Artistic environments must be able to work with and motivate workers who can be emotional and temperamental.

## Pitfalls

The minimal structure found in Artistic environments can lead to disorder, disarray and disorganization, as everyone (in an extreme example) does things as they prefer, move at their own pace and in accord with their own whims. Essentially, Artistic environments can produce some real inconsistencies in terms of work methods, decision making and procedures.

While the sense of excitement and energy is palpable in Artistic environments when things are going well and new projects succeed, they can become gloomy, frustrating and depressing when ideas are not flowing or gaining acceptance within the larger organization. Similarly, individuals within Artistic environments can be moody and emotional. If the leader of such an Artistic group has such a personality, their team's performance may well mirror their moods. This can result in many ups and downs for the group as a whole, along with considerable frustration and tension.

Since the creative process is largely intuitive or instinctive, Artistic environments can lack a certain amount of pragmatism, common sense and logic. Ideas that sound great at first glance may be implemented and developed fully, only to discover at a late date, an important piece of data or objective information was overlooked or underrated. This can result in considerable wasted time, energy and effort.

If an Artistic environment is part of a larger organization that is not characterized by this Holland theme, resentment can arise when others discover the freedoms the Artistic group has, compared to themselves. The temperamental and "undisciplined" nature of Artistic environments can also conflict with the business-oriented aspects of larger organizations. Not surprisingly, members of Artistic environments may lack a facility for managing the bottom line or financial aspects of their operations.

## Leadership

Artistic environments *define* flexible leadership. That is, leaders in these environments foster an open atmosphere where ideas are freely expressed, risks are taken and experimentation is rewarded. In this regard, people working in such environments are encouraged to think beyond the norm and are reinforced for doing so. Roles in Artistic environments are frequently informal and changeable, rather than definite and distinct. This is often necessary and workable because of the project-based nature of the work, and the need for personnel to change roles as the occasion arises. Typically, there is no clear or rigid chain of command in Artistic environments either. This usually results in leaders who are accessible and approachable. Goals in these environments are loosely defined, which allows freedom to make midstream adjustments when necessary.

The inherent flexibility of Artistic environments can result in leadership that is overly relaxed or laissez-faire. This, then can foster a lack of discipline in some workers. In addition, Artistic leaders can place too much faith in the hands of individuals who are not wholly dependable nor proven talents. Likewise, direction from leaders in these environments sometimes occurs in fits and starts as goals and objectives are changed unexpectedly.

# CHAPTER 27

◆

# SOCIAL ENVIRONMENTS: "ARE YOU SERVICE-ORIENTED?"

**What they are like**

The Social environment is attuned to the needs and feelings of people working within it. It is nurturing, caring and warm. Workers in Social environments generally have a sense of security flowing from the concern shown for their welfare. In fact, there is often a family-oriented atmosphere in Social environments reflected in a close-knit group of workers.

The structure in these environments is built around relationships. Specifically, there are often rules of conduct—unspoken or not, but understood—that are adhered to by all. Conflict is avoided or handled with great tact and discretion, compromise is encouraged, and the needs of all are taken into account when decisions are made.

In Social environments, goals and expectations are reasonably clear and frequently left open to discussion. Yet, in some aspects, goals can also be vague. An example would be a provision that all workers provide sound service to customers, which is quite general, and open to individual inter-pretation. Despite this, people in Social environments are usually careful in completing their work and in handling details.

Because workers in Social environments want to please their managers and customers, there is apt to be consistency regarding service levels and performance over time. Goals in these environments are seldom exceed-ingly challenging or overly strenuous to attain. This is not to suggest Social environments are pressure free. In fact, there can be a great deal of pressure in Social environments due to the extensive people interaction occurring within them, and the potential that brings for interpersonal conflict.

Oftentimes, within Social environments, individuals are left much room for discretion in terms of when they will complete certain tasks or responsibilities. That is, deadlines may not always be hard-and-fast. Furthermore, across groups and functions, there is usually a good deal of communication and cooperation as everyone pulls together to reach mutual goals. In this sense, Social environments often involve or demand a high level of inter-dependency among groups.

Social environments are normally low-risk environments where taking chances is not critical to success. Actually, taking risks in Social environ-ments could have significant and profoundly negative "impacts" because others' health, welfare or well-being could be jeopardized. Consequently, playing things safe is encouraged overtly or quietly. This can also result in decisions being made relatively slowly in Social environments. This is especially true if others might be hurt, offended or otherwise negatively affected by these decisions.

## Nature of the work

The work undertaken in Social environments is helping-oriented and service-based. These environments naturally consist of a considerable amount of people interaction. Personnel in Social environments provide assistance, help, guidance and encouragement to others (e.g., customer service representatives, vocational counselors, nurses). Frequently, there is a teaching or training aspect to the work being done in these environments. There is also a need for strong human relations skills because of the frequent interpersonal interactions involved in the work being done. Conflict resolution can be a part of the work that occurs in Social environments because Social types have a natural ability for smoothing over differences and encouraging others to talk about issues of concern while defusing any attendant anger.

## What is rewarded?

Social environments value cooperation, tolerance and friendliness. The ability to work effectively with others is essential. This is especially true since Social environments are normally people-intensive and coworkers have to work closely (psychologically, at least), with each other or with customers or clients or patients. Responsiveness to others' needs or requirements is equally vital. Empathy and sympathy are values or qualities that are highly important in these environments as well.

The ability to communicate orally is critical in Social environments as this is a primary means for sharing important information. Flowing from this, a facility for "networking" within Social environments is considered crucial when it comes to organizational planning and decision making. Generally, Social environments allow room for informal channels of communication to develop that can be useful to management in "testing the waters" with new ideas, programs, policies, et cetera. Similarly, asking questions is reinforced in Social environments as this allows for better understanding among coworkers and different groups or departments.

## Getting Ahead

Advancement in Social environments is earned through a number of means. One has to do with a person's ability to get along well with other personnel. This includes possessing a skill for gaining others' support in working toward group goals. A second basis for advancing in Social environments has to do with knowing how to motivate a team of individuals, resolving conflict among associates and maintaining positive morale. A third important criteria for getting ahead in Social environments revolves around a person's facility for teaching, training and instructing others. A fourth attribute that will help a person advance within Social environments is the ability to manage upward, lateral and downward relationships without alienating anyone in the process. Finally, people in Social environments will enhance their likelihood of advancing if they are effective handling disciplinary matters without being too easygoing and tenderhearted.

## Pitfalls

Social environments can fail to be sufficiently results-oriented. Too much time and attention can be focused on the people side of the "equation." This can result in procrastination, slow progress on projects, and a lack of adherence to time requirements or deadlines.

Conflict or true differences of opinion can be glossed over in Social environments. This can lead to situations where frustration along with bad or ill feelings are kept inside rather than shared with appropriate personnel. Unfortunately, these types of negative feelings may come out unexpectedly, in an emotional outburst, some time in the future well after the original event.

People within Social environments may, too frequently, take the safe route when making decisions or avoid making tough, painful choices that are necessary to achieve a goal. In this regard, bottom line considerations can be overlooked when it comes to business decisions. Social environments can be overly protective of workers, which can stifle their growth and development. As a result, some individuals or groups within Social environments may underachieve. Goals and expectations may not be sufficiently challenging or realistic. In addition, meetings in Social environments can be protracted affairs where too much idle talking occurs and not enough "meaningful" discussion takes place. This can lead to the appearance of action in the form of earnest talk, but no resolution of problems.

## Leadership

Social environments produce leadership that is caring, generous, extremely fair and tolerant. There is often much in the way of positive feedback, support, encouragement and appreciation provided in these environments. Furthermore, workers in Social environments usually have a voice in decisions affecting them, reflecting a participative style of management. Leaders in these environments always consider the impact their decisions will have on the people around them. Although such consideration is often appreciated, it can lead to leaders who avoid making unpopular decisions.

Leaders in Social environments are non-directive or mildly directive, but never harsh or dictatorial. Instead, they rely on empathy, friendliness and compassion to win over those they lead and get the best out of them. Unfortunately, leaders in Social environments can be too sympathetic, patient and understanding. This can result in putting off tackling personnel and performance problems, and being too lenient when they do address them. Because such leaders believe strongly in the power of positive recognition and are non-confrontive, they avoid delivering criticism or saying anything to workers that might hurt or offend even when such feedback is justified.

Social environments can become too relaxed and encourage a laissez-faire approach to managing people. When this occurs, workers can be given too much autonomy and freedom without sufficient accountability.

# CHAPTER 28

◆

# ENTERPRISING ENVIRONMENTS: "WHAT HAVE YOU DONE FOR US LATELY?"

**What they are like**

The Enterprising environment is goal-oriented and the structure that exists consists of those essential elements needed to reach objectives. That is, guidelines are established upon answering the question, "Will this rule or procedure further everyone's ability to meet the organizations needs?" If the answer is "Yes," it will be implemented. Despite this, guidelines are rarely absolute in Enterprising environments. Instead, there is a good deal of flexibility and room for interpretation left to individuals in these environments. To a certain extent, in Enterprising environments, guidelines are followed or not, depending upon the demand of the moment—if it is *expedient* to bypass a rule to further a goal or exceed it, then so be it.

Enterprising environments definitely encourage risk taking and a venturesome spirit. Individuals within such environments can earn plenty of freedom to take gambles—provided they are successful most of the time. This indicates that calculated risks or chances taken, based upon sound information or experience, are preferable to pure gambling, which is true. Enterprising environments also demand that individuals be forward looking and logical when making decisions. In light of the above, Enterprising environments certainly welcome innovation and change. Yet, the important factor in determining whether a change is implemented or not revolves around its ability to positively influence profits.

Not surprisingly, Enterprising environments are high-pressure environments where job security is based upon the question, "What have you done for us lately?" There is not much tolerance for failing to achieve objectives. Criticism is provided to all personnel in a direct fashion, and the implementation of tough discipline for subpart performance is swift.

## Nature of the work

Work in Enterprising environments is focused on the strategic needs of the organization and the overall picture. Personnel operating in these environments devote the bulk of their attention to long-range planning and broader operational issues. Likewise, decisions that affect the organization as a whole, are of key importance and those of a day-to-day nature are delegated to others.

Enterprising environments are not places where fine attention to detail is looked upon as vital to success. This flows, in part, from the fact that these environments are frequently fast paced, energetic—even exciting—places where the ability to juggle multiple demands is more important than being precise, accurate and thorough. So, a certain room for error is accepted. In this regard, Enterprising environments oftentimes are established or organized in such a way that there are other workers (other than Enterprising types) who manage or fill in the fine details, while the Enterprising individuals attend to the bigger picture. As this suggests, the willingness to take charge is important in Enterprising environments.

## What is rewarded?

Enterprising environments value the ability to deliver outstanding results, which entail risk taking, a competitive drive and lots of ambition. In fact, Enterprising environments consist of ambitious people, all eager to make their mark on the organization and move up to ever-increasing levels of responsibility. Prestige, status and power are highly desirable elements of Enterprising environments wherein a person's position, placement on the organizational chart or degree of authority are means of readily determining a person's value.

Enterprising environments value aggressiveness, boldness and a willingness to stand up and fight for what you believe in. These attributes demand the ability to be fast on one's feet, and confidence to continue pressing for an idea or proposal in the face of opposition. Enterprising environments also prize leadership, or the ability to take charge, develop a clear vision, get a team focused, and see a project or goal through to a successful completion. Another valued attribute in Enterprising environments is tenacity or an unwillingness to quit in the face of long odds or difficult circumstances.

## Getting Ahead

Advancement in Enterprising environments is earned through a number of means. One has to do with consistently exceeding goals and expectations. Note that merely meeting established goals may not be enough to get ahead. A second important basis for moving up in Enterprising environments relates to a person's ability to take risks and succeed in spite of obstacles, problems, barriers, et cetera that arise. The larger the risk, the stronger the impact on the success of the organization, the faster a person's rise in that organization. Enterprising environments are not at all adverse to promoting successful, but relatively youthful individuals. A third criteria for getting ahead in Enterprising environments revolves around the strength or forcefulness of a person's personality. Assertive, dominating types of people will advance quickly compared to amiable people, all other things being equal. A fourth attribute that contributes to moving up in Enterprising environments has to do with one's skill in motivating others to follow their lead, and work hard to reach objectives. Finally, people in Enterprising environments will noticeably enhance their likelihood of advancing if they demonstrate a sense of dedication that goes well beyond that of their peers. That is, Enterprising environments require those who advance to prove they have much more than an average commitment to their work as demonstrated in their willingness to put in very long hours.

## Pitfalls

It is not unusual for Enterprising environments to become political environments where different groups or individuals look out too much for their own interests, versus the greater good. A climate of distrust or suspicion regarding others' motives can ensue. This can further result in "power struggles" among these groups or individuals. The "losers" in these battles are usually forced out of the organization along with people identified as their "followers" or sympathizers.

Change can occur too quickly in some Enterprising environments. This flows from the risk-taking nature of these environments, as well as the impatience for action and propensity to sometimes act (or react) too quickly to changes in the marketplace, the economy, or those made by outside competition. In these situations, the lack of attention to details paid by Es can result in decisions that make a certain amount of sense from an overall perspective, but reveal a lack of in-depth planning and attention to tactical issues.

Enterprising environments can develop into "up or out" organizations where employee turnover is high. This sort of mindset can downplay the importance of steady, dependable, but unspectacular performers, who are necessary to solidifying departments and providing continuity.

**Leadership**

The style of management found in Enterprising environments leans toward being autocratic, "top-down," hierarchical, driving and aggressive. Expectations for others in Enterprising environments are high and competitiveness is encouraged as a means of getting the best out of everyone. Recognition and rewards are earned based on each person's bottom-line contribution to the organization. The more you contribute, the more recognition you receive, and the greater your rewards—usually, financial. Enterprising environments may also establish a variety of different incentives to encourage continuous performance improvement. Greater independence, opportunities for advancement and other "perks" are granted to the strongest performers in Enterprising environments.

Leaders in Enterprising environments take an overall view of their responsibilities and develop a clear, long-term vision of what they want to achieve. They communicate this to their team and continually challenge everyone to excel. Such leaders are strategic thinkers with an ability to understand the bigger picture. They often see opportunities where others see problems or obstacles. In addition, they have an ability to sell their vision to others, rally their team, and get everyone pointed in the direction they need to reach their goals. Leaders in Enterprising environments delegate freely, hold people accountable, and are swift to confront anyone falling short of expectations.

Unfortunately, some Enterprising environments can be so driving, demanding and results focused that people may be treated with little or no compassion or empathy. This can result in an environment where workers become overly concerned about the possibility of not reaching a goal for fear of being disciplined or fired. There can also be a notable lack of warmth, encouragement and support from management, and too much in the way of critical feedback when mistakes are made or goals are not attained. Coworkers may fail to cooperate with each other because competition can become less than friendly and even unhealthy. Thus, these environments can be undone as a consequence of unfettered competition, unbridled ambition and too much pressure to perform placed on leaders and, in turn, their teams.

# CHAPTER 29

◆

# CONVENTIONAL ENVIRONMENTS: "CAN YOU DEVELOP EFFICIENT PROCEDURES?"

**What they are like**

The Conventional environment is organized around clear, specific rules, policies and procedures. There is little in the way of ambiguity; and, there is often little room for interpretation when it comes to established standards. Work proceeds in a well-ordered fashion wherein every worker knows their role as well as the limits of their authority and responsibility. Conventional environments are characterized by a good deal of predictability and consistency so that it is rare for an exception to be made regarding rules and operating procedures.

The pace within Conventional environments is usually moderate, but seldom hectic for long periods of time. Although, certain Conventional environments can have times of the year when demands pick up considerably for weeks or a few months at a time. The rules and procedures inherent in Conventional environments can help to contribute a calmness that is reflected in a polite informality among coworkers. Generally speaking, Conventional environments possess a low keyed or quiet atmosphere.

Conventional environments are often clean, neat, even hygienic environments where everything seems to have and be in its proper place. To an outsider, workers in Conventional environments would appear efficient, persevering, disciplined and cooperative while they work with each other to reach mutual goals.

## Nature of the work

The work taking place in Conventional environments is typically detail oriented, well defined and very structured. As well, there are often high standards established regarding the accuracy, precision and quality of work produced. Within Conventional environments, there is little tolerance for disarray, inefficiency or disorganization. Furthermore, work in Conventional environments entail careful and systematic collection, manipulation and reproduction of different types of data. This would include such activities as maintaining records, filing, ordering materials and operating business equipment (e.g., copiers, computers, facsimile equipment, et cetera). In addition, any work or activity that is clerical could take place in a Conventional environment.

## What is rewarded?

Conventional environments value accuracy and precision. As such, strong perceptual skills are important. Conventional environments also place a premium on efficiency. Therefore, workers within Conventional environments are usually effective at establishing sensible routines or procedures that eliminate disorder or wasted time. Quality in one's work is considered a key requirement in Conventional environments, and can help ensure a person's security.

Another attribute that is reinforced in Conventional environments is cautiousness. This would be evidenced in a worker being patient in completing tasks and assignments, even those that are tedious or repetitive. Cautiousness would also be reflected in a lack or haste or impulsiveness when making decisions and a willingness to ask for help when needed to avoid errors or mistakes.

Courtesy is an important quality that is needed to operate successfully within Conventional environments. This includes the ability to work effectively with other team members, and respect for the authority and decisions of superiors. Conventional environments also place an emphasis on following the chain of command.

Conventional environments certainly place a premium on strong implementation skills. They also emphasize the ability to meet one's obligations without complaint or being confrontational. The latter qualities, (i.e., a lack of aggressiveness) are a requisite element in ensuring the work demanded of Conventional environments is completed properly and without undue delay.

## Getting Ahead

Advancement in Conventional environments is earned through a number of means. One has to do with respecting guidelines and policies and ensuring others do not stray from these. Thus, individuals who ensure that the "glue" of the organization is maintained will be looked upon favorably. A second basis for moving up in Conventional environments has to do with a person's awareness of the organization's bottom-line needs, and making efficient use of its monetary resources. A third valuable attribute is longevity. That is, individuals who are long-tenured compared to other employees will enhance their chances of taking on additional responsibility in the future. A fourth means of earning the chance to step up in Conventional environments revolves around being able to develop cost-saving ideas, or efficient and *obvious* enhancements to procedures or policies, or refinements in those that catch the attention of superiors. Finally, advancing within Conventional environments can be enhanced by becoming affiliated with a manager who is viewed as a solid contributor (or a "rising star"), and maintaining a strong relationship with that person.

## Pitfalls

When the emphasis on following rules becomes extreme, Conventional environments can become bureaucratic. As this occurs, work and decisions can proceed at a frustratingly slow pace. The layers that decisions must pass through that once made sense, can take on a life of their own and represent a waste of time and energy—not to mention frustration to those who must wait for action. These same rules hinder or eliminate the possibility of risk taking, innovation and creativity on the part of people within Conventional environments. In fact, Conventional environments can be quietly resistant to change represented by a passive-aggressive approach to preventing or stifling it.

Workers within Conventional environments can become overly concerned with details to the point where non-critical tasks are overworked or standards for accuracy are set at unrealistically high levels. This can result in workers feeling they are unable to meet these standards on a regular basis, thereby creating unnecessary anxiety or frustration. A keen focus on details can leave Conventional workers blind to the broader picture, and result in their being too short-termed focused when planning or making decisions.

Conventional environments are often lacking in people possessing assertiveness. For this reason, no one may want to "stick their neck out" and make a tough decision, or fight for their rights. Consequently, workers in Conventional environments can find their needs, interests and feelings overlooked or unsatisfied. Such individuals may feel frustrated that their accomplishments are not acknowledged, and their careers do not advance as hoped. Along with this, there can be a dearth of "true" leadership within Conventional environments and adherence to procedures and rules can become a de facto substitute for it.

## Leadership

Among departments or different areas within Conventional environments, there exist definite lines of demarcation. For this reason, decision-making responsibility and authority are well distributed (or splintered), so no one person has overall authority—except, of course, top managers—for making significant decisions. Consequently, broad or far-reaching decisions may be broken down in such a way that several different people or areas are responsible for discrete aspects of the larger decision. This can tend to create "layers" within Conventional environments that demand a series of approvals for definite action to occur. It is also a way of building safeguards into the organization to prevent the abuse of authority or too much power being centered within the hands of a few individuals. An unfortunate side effect of this layering is sometimes a bureaucratic mind-set that, despite the normal efficiency of the Conventional type, leads to just the opposite end result. Thus, rules and procedures can inexplicably become ends in themselves.

Leaders in Conventional environments are believers in the chain of command and the notion that advancement should take place based on tenure and seniority. Thus, while Conventional types often want to get ahead, they do believe it is necessary to work hard, put in their time and wait their turn. Leaders in these environments strive to stay on top and in control of work being done by their team. As such, they maintain a focus on day-to-day demands and activities. Consequently, Conventional leaders are tactically-oriented, but not strategic in their outlook. Beyond this, they tend to supervise other's work closely, thereby ensuring accuracy and proper adherence to procedures. A negative aspect to this behavior is it can result in  controlling and over-supervising work under their direction.

# CHAPTER 30

$\blacklozenge$

# CREATING A PICTURE OF YOUR IDEAL WORK ENVIRONMENT

This chapter is designed to help you define the optimal work environment to pursue based upon your Holland scores on the self-tests from chapters 1 through 6. If you have not yet completed the self-tests, do so now and return to this chapter.

Complete the following exercises according to the instructions provided. Read through them carefully

Exercise 1: Utilizing information from your highest Holland-theme score.

*Step One*

My highest Holland score from the self-tests is for the _____ theme. (If there was a tie for your two highest theme scores, complete steps one through three for *each* theme.)

## Step Two

Refer to the appropriate section of chapter 24-29 where the work environment for your highest theme listed above is described. Read through the entire description of that Holland work environment.

## Step Three

Re-read the same section of the above chapter. But, this time, as you read, highlight, underline or otherwise note those parts of the description you feel are important elements you want to see in your work environment.

## Exercise 2: Utilizing information from your second-highest Holland-theme score.

## Step One

My second-highest Holland score from the self-test is for the: theme.

## Step Two

Refer to the section of chapter 24-29 where the work environment for your second-highest theme listed above is described. Read through the entire description of that Holland work environment.

## Step Three

Re-read the same section of chapter 24-29. But, this time, as you read, highlight, underline or otherwise note those parts of the description you feel are important elements you want to see in your work environment.

<u>Exercise 3: Summarizing the information from Exercises 1 & 2.</u>

In this exercise, you will organize the information you highlighted while completing Exercises 1 and 2. You will do this by classifying all of the information as top, middle and low-level priorities. This "ranking" will then represent those things you believe to be important elements in your work environment.

Under the appropriate headings below, write down the information you highlighted while completing Exercises 1 & 2.

<u>*Step 1*</u>

The following are *important* attributes, values, elements, people-qualities, et cetera, for me in a work environment. I *must* have most of these wherever I am employed, as they are *top-level priorities:*

## Step 2

The following are *relatively* important attributes, values, elements, people-qualities, et cetera, for me in a work environment. I am willing to make some trade-offs in these areas, as they are *middle-level priorities*:

## *Step 3*

The following are attributes, values, elements, people-qualities, et cetera, that would be *nice to have* in a work environment. These, along with those listed in steps 1 & 2, would represent an *ideal* work setting for me. Because of this, I can, if necessary, live without many of the items listed below and view these as *low-level priorities:*

•

## Step 4

When you are at the point in your job search where you are looking for potential places of employment, discussing your career needs with a recruiter, or interviewing for positions with organizations, keep the above information handy. Refer to it as a checklist while you evaluate different potential employers as to their suitability in satisfying *your* unique work environment needs. This information can be invaluable when you are being considered for a position by an organization. Use it to probe representatives of companies or outside recruiters during interviews they conduct with you. When they ask, "Do you have any questions?" use this checklist to ascertain their ability to satisfy your top, middle and low level priorities. Also, refer to these priorities when negotiating your employment "package," using it to make possible trade-offs with your future employer where feasible.

# EPILOGUE

———◆———

There you have it! John Holland's theory of interests, personality and careers. I hope you have found this information illuminating, while learning more about yourself, the people around you, and your preferred work environment.

If you used this book to learn about your personality, strengths and shortcomings, apply the information you gleaned to fully employ your current skills and abilities. At the same time, focus on how you can improve your weaker areas. These goals can be accomplished by creating a developmental action plan. This plan should outline activities you can engage in to fully utilize your existing strengths, while including activities to help you develop in areas needing improvement. When creating your plan, set clear, specific goals and timetables, identify people who can assist you, and regularly measure your progress while making necessary midstream adjustments to your plan.

If you used this book to discover a more satisfying job or career, be sure to periodically review the information you compiled when developing your personal profile and ideal work environment. Use it as indicated when you conduct a job search. In addition, be sure to use the resources available to you at the local library, college or university. Visit the career/vocational sections of the library or talk to a counselor to learn about your career needs, interests and requirements. Do not hesitate to employ the services of a career counselor who maintains a private practice. Finally, make use of the extensive career information available on the internet. For example, many college counseling centers have web sites that are accessible through their university's web site. All of these sources, along with those listed in the bibliography, can be of tremendous assistance in your pursuit of a satisfying career.

If you used this book to do a better job managing people, keep it handy as a resource to turn to when you run into a coworker or employee you are having difficulty motivating or understanding. Begin the process of learning about them by determining their primary and secondary Holland types (refer to chapters 1 through 6). Once you have these identified, you can gain a clearer picture by considering which pair of themes best describes them (refer to chapters 8 through 22). Consider how you may need to adjust your own interpersonal style to better relate to or motivate these individuals.

Good luck to you in your endeavors!

# About the Author

━━━━━━━━━━━━━━━━ ◆ ━━━━━━━━━━━━━━━━

During high school, Mr. Juchnowski (pronounced, JUCK-NOW-SKI) did not know what he wanted to do upon graduation. He demonstrated good math skills and an interest in the sciences, which resulted in guidance counselors suggesting he pursue accounting in college. He enrolled in a community college and duly signed up for business math and accounting classes. He excelled in the math course, hated accounting and dropped out of school before the end of his first quarter. Not surprisingly, discouragement followed, as did a three-year stint as a production worker in a window factory—and, further discouragement. By chance, at this point in his misery, Mr. Juchnowski applied for and received a position working for a chemical company. He was now a lab worker, growing inorganic crystals used in high tech applications, (e.g., infrared detectors, CAT scanners). He loved the lab work and excelled at the scientific part of his job. This fueled his interest in taking a second stab at college, which he did at Cleveland State University (CSU). He was also part of, and eventually became an officer in the local chemical worker's union.

Mr. Juchnowski worked during the day and attended college at night with his mind set on earning a bachelor's degree in chemistry. Unfortunately, he became disenchanted with the continual union-management fighting and decided to make a job change. He accepted a position with a different chemical company, continued growing crystals and was charged with establishing and supervising an entirely new crystal growth process for this organization—which he did successfully. Mr. Juchnowski also continued his studies at CSU, but found his interest in chemistry waning, and replaced by a stronger interest in psychology. In the end, he switched his major to psychology, earned an undergraduate degree in this field, was laid-off from his job, and immediately enrolled in a graduate program at CSU focusing on consumer and industrial psychology. After earning a master's degree, Mr. Juchnowski began a new career as a human resources consultant.

All told, Mr. Juchnowski worked in the chemical industry for thirteen years, and has been a consultant for the last fifteen. It took him ten years to earn his undergraduate degree. Currently, he directs Strategic Decisions, an organization that provides training, services and products to help organizations assess job candidates, maximize the potential of employees, and career counseling to individuals. Strategic Decisions is based in northeast Ohio, near Cleveland. Its e-mail address is: strategic1@earthlink.net.

Mr. Juchnowski's Holland code is IRS. Coincidentally (or not), the fields of chemistry and psychology each fall within the Holland Investigative theme.

# BIBLIOGRAPHY

Gottfredson, G.D. and Holland, J.L. *Dictionary of occupational Holland codes*. 2nd ed. Odessa, Florida: Psychological Assessment Resources, 1989.

JIST Works, Inc. *The enhanced guide for occupational exploration*. Indianapolis, Indiana: JIST Works, Inc., 1991.

Holland, J.L. *The self-directed search professional manual*. Odessa, Florida: Psychological Assessment Resources, 1985.

Holland, J.L. *The manual supplement for the self-directed search*. Odessa, Florida: Psychological Assessment Resources, 1987.

Holland, J.L. *Making vocational choices*. 3rd ed. Odessa, Florida: Psychological Assessment Resources, 1997.

Lowman, R.L. *The clinical practice of career assessment*. Washington, D.C.: American Psychological Association, 1991.

Montross, Leibowitz and Shinkman. *Real people real jobs*. Palo Alto, California: Davies-Black Publishing, 1995.

Shahnasarian, M. *The self-directed search (SDS) in business and industry*. Odessa, Florida: Psychological Assessment Resources, 1996.

U.S. Department of Labor. *Occupational outlook handbook 2000–2001*. Indianapolis, Indiana: JIST Works, Inc., 2000.

# INDEX

CPSIA information can be obtained at www.ICGtesting.com
Printed in the USA
LVOW06s0530090114

368713LV00001B/171/A